Whether you're just beginning your new life as a married couple or are well along on your journey together, *Partners for Life* is a book that will enrich and enhance your lives, helping you to move toward the goal of oneness that God has established for you.

Your marriage does not have to be in crisis to benefit from this in-depth study. Whatever the situation in your marriage, there is always room for growth and improvement. Gene and Elaine Getz will help you explore and discover more about your mate, yourself, and your unique relationship together. Through personal example, study of the Word of God, and practical, personalized worksheets, you will move into fresh and exciting dimensions of this beautiful, mysterious bonding we call marriage.

Partners for Life

Partners for Life

Making a Marriage that Lasts

GENE & ELAINE GETZ

Regal Books

A Division of GL Publications
Ventura, California, U.S.A.

Published by Regal Books
A Division of Gospel Light
Ventura, California, U.S.A.
Printed in U.S.A.

Library of Congress Cataloging-in-Publication Data

Getz, Gene A.
　　　　Partners for life : making a marriage that lasts / by Gene and Elaine
Getz.
　　　　　　p.　　　　　　　　cm.—(the biblical renewal series)
　　　　Bibliography: p.
　　　　ISBN 0-8307-1306-9
　　　　1. Marriage—Religious aspects—Christianity. I. Getz, Elaine. II Getz,
Gene A. Biblical renewal series. III. Title.
BV835.G48　　　1988　　　　　　　　　　　　　　88-15798
248.8'4—dc19　　　　　　　　　　　　　　　　　　CIP

5　6　7　8　9　10　11　12　13　14　15　16　17　/　00　99　98　97　96　95　94

Rights for publishing this book in other languages are contracted by Gospel Literature International (GLINT). GLINT also provides technical help for the adaptation, translation, and publishing of Bible study resources and books in scores of languages worldwide. For further information, contact GLINT, Post Office Box 4060, Ontario, California, 91761-1003, U.S.A., or the publisher.

CONTENTS

RENEWAL:
A BIBLICAL
PERSPECTIVE

Renewal is the essence of dynamic Christianity and the basis on which Christians, both in a corporate or "body" sense and as individual believers, can determine the will of God. Paul made this clear when he wrote to the Roman Christians—"be transformed by the *renewing of your mind.* Then," he continued, "you will be able to test and approve what God's will is" (Rom. 12:2). Here Paul is talking about renewal in both a personal and a corporate sense. In other words, Paul is asking these Christians as a *body* of believers to develop the mind of Christ through corporate renewal.

Personal renewal will not happen as God intended it

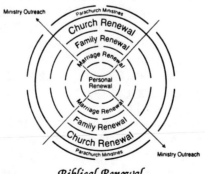

Biblical Renewal

unless it happens in the context of corporate renewal. On the other hand, corporate renewal will not happen as God intended without personal renewal. Both are necessary.

The larger circle represents "church renewal." This is the most comprehensive concept in the New Testament. However, every local church is made up of smaller self-contained, but interrelated units. The *family* in Scripture emerges as the "church in miniature." In turn, the family is made up of an even smaller social unit—*marriage.* The third inner circle represents *personal* renewal, which is inseparably linked to all of the other basic units. Marriage is made up of two separate individuals who become one. The family is made up of parents and children who are also to reflect the mind of Christ. And the church is made up of not only individual Christians, but couples and families.

Though all of these social units are interrelated, biblical renewal can begin within any specific social unit. But wherever it begins—in the church, families, marriages or individuals—the process immediately touches all the other social units. And one thing is certain! All that God says is consistent and harmonious. He does not have one set of principles for the Church and another set for the family, another for husbands and wives, and another for individual Christians. For example, the principles God outlines for local church elders, fathers and husbands, regarding their role as leaders, are interrelated and consistent. If they are not, we can be sure that we have not interpreted God's plan accurately.

The Biblical Renewal Series is an expanding library of books by Gene Getz designed to provide supportive help in moving toward renewal. Each of these books fits into one of the circles described above and will provoke thought, provide interaction and tangible steps toward growth. You will find a detailed listing of the Biblical Renewal Series titles at the back of this book.

HOW TO USE
THIS BOOK
(A Letter from the Authors)

Dear Friends,

It's a privilege for us to share this material with you. It has grown out of our own experience and our growth together as a married couple and through our conducting classes and seminars for others. We trust you'll enjoy it as much as we have. Allow us, however, to give you some suggestions on how to use this book.

As an Individual

Though we designed this book first and foremost for use by a married couple, you can also use it as a single person contemplating marriage. And even if you're married and your mate is not interested in this study, you can gain helpful insights for yourself that will assist you greatly in growing together with your marital partner. Simply work through the projects designed for you and learn all you can.

As a Couple

This book is a do-it-yourself marriage enrichment course. Initially, read the introductory material in each chapter. Then, together, work through the projects step-by-step.

You have three options for using this book as a couple:

First, purchase two copies of the book. This is the preferable way to use this material, which will enable each of you as a marital partner to have a copy. This way you can read the introductory material in each chapter at your convenience, you can underscore certain ideas, you can make notes and then each of you can work through your own exercises and projects.

Second, you can duplicate one set of exercises on a copy machine. You have our permission to do so, thus enabling you to keep your book intact.

Third, you can remove the perforated sheets designed for you and place them in a separate notebook. Understand, of course, that if you take this approach, you will disassemble the book.

As a Group of Couples

This material is also designed to be used with a group of couples. We have prepared a set of videotapes (four hours), *The Dynamics of a Successful Marriage,* that will assist you in using this material in a class setting. You'll be able to use these videos both in preparation and in leading the seminar or in teaching the classes. This course may also be used by an individual.

Marriage Counseling

We've also found this material to be very effective in marriage counseling. Simply have each partner work through the projects prior to coming into the counseling sessions. If these assignments are taken seriously, you will be amazed at how much progress you can make in the counseling process.

May we say in closing, that as a couple we have conducted a number of seminars, refining this material over a period of time. Also, we have developed a very effective group process which is explained in the forthcoming leader's guide. Our prayer is that this material will enrich your marriage as it has ours, and that it will help you help others to do the same.

Growing together,
Gene and Elaine Getz
Dallas, Texas

INTRODUCTION
Let's Grow Together

Partners for Life is a course for every couple, no matter how long you've been married or where you are in your relationship with one another. Generally, marriage is like any human relationship. There's always room for enrichment, renewal and growth. More specifically, however, marriage offers an opportunity for growth in ways other relationships do not. Being married opens the door to experiencing oneness at an ever increasing level. Because of the uniqueness of this relationship, it enables a man and woman to understand in unusual ways what it means to be made in the image of God. Because men and women are created in God's image, there is always more to learn about each other. Just as we will never know all there is to know about God, we will never be able to know all there is to know about each other in any given lifetime.

We have been married for over 30 years. Our three children are grown and have virtually left the nest. In some respects, we wondered what it would be like to face this time in our lives—especially when the youngest was about to leave for college. True, we experienced many of the emotions that go along with the "empty nest" syndrome; we're very close to our children. But, somewhat unexpectedly, we both experienced a new sense of freedom to concentrate more on our growth together as a married couple. In some respects, we feel we're just beginning.

So join us—and let's all "grow together" in this marvelous and mysterious relationship God calls marriage (see Eph. 5:31,32).

Gene and Elaine Getz

1

BECOMING ONE

Today, for various reasons, most marriages are undergoing some degree of stress. All human relationships experience strain due to the realities of life. Marriage represents the most intimate human relationship of all, and is probably affected more than any other by those very realities. Consequently, every marriage undergoes degrees of stress.

However, there is a more specific reason all marriages experience stress. Our present-day societal structures are groaning and creaking from various changes that are continually bombarding our cultural foundations. Since every marriage is an integral part of the total culture, these changes—philosophical, moral, economic and technological—all affect society in general and marriages in particular.

Dr. Allan Bloom, speaking of marriage in his blockbuster volume entitled *The Closing of the American Mind*, states that "the decomposition of this bond is surely America's most urgent social problem. But," he continues, "nobody ever tries to do anything about it. The tide seems irreversible. Among the many items on the agenda of those promoting America's moral regeneration, I never find marriage and divorce."[1]

Writing from both a semi-religious and secular perspective, Bloom hit the nail on the head. But, thank God, as Christians, we *can* do something about this trend in our society—beginning with our own marriages. And this, perhaps, will be our greatest gift to our children, who face deteriorating marital structures in our society, which Bloom considers an irreversible trend. As believers, we can be "in the world," and yet "not part of it"—providing we look at God's guidelines and principles for marriage and, with God's help, commit ourselves to applying these principles day by day.

In Paul's letter to the Ephesians, he quoted both Moses and Jesus when he stated, "For this cause a man shall leave his father and mother, and shall cleave to his wife; and *the two shall become one flesh*"[2] (Eph. 5:31; see also Gen. 2:24, Matt. 19:5,6). F. Foulkes has written that "this statement from the creation story is the most profound and fundamental statement in the whole of Scripture concerning God's plan for marriage."[3]

One in Humanness

How was "oneness" illustrated in the original creation? When God first created Adam, there was no one with whom he could truly become "one flesh." There was no other human being with whom he could share his life. The implication is clear. It would take another person created in God's image—and Adam's image—to fill that unique role. This is what God meant when He said that He would make a "helper *suitable*" (Gen. 2:18). This literally means "a help of his life," that is, "a helping being, which, as soon as he sees it, he may recognize himself."[4] This is why Adam exclaimed when he first saw Eve, "This is now bone of my bones, and flesh of my flesh; She shall be called Woman, Because she was taken out of Man" (Gen. 2:23).

Adam recognized that Eve was like him. Though she was uniquely female, she looked like him, talked like him, walked like him and smiled like him. She was his complement. He could relate to her as to no other living creature. She was another human being.

One in Sexuality

Eve was indeed one with Adam because she was literally taken from his side. Part of his very physical body became part of Eve's physical body. And before they were ever joined together sexually, they were already, in God's eyes, one flesh.

On the other hand, what caused a man and woman to become one flesh in God's eyes after the original creation? First, we must understand that there is a unique relationship between *all* men and women. Ever since God created the first man and woman, every male and female reflect the same unity. Together, both men and women are made in God's image (see Gen. 1:27). And together we reflect His image and His creative handiwork.

God's perfect will is that it be a permanent relationship, involving one man and one woman, reflecting the original creation.

But, as we all know, there is an even more unique relationship that God intended. Though He certainly planned for all human beings (both male and female) to fellowship with one another and to relate to one another because of the ongoing oneness inherent in the original creation, there is yet another oneness referred to in Scripture—the oneness that exists between a husband and a wife who join together in sexual intercourse. In this God-created consummation, the original creation is illustrated again and again throughout history. In God's eyes, a man and woman become one flesh and continue to reflect this one flesh relationship in this God-ordained experience.

One in Spirituality

Part of the great mystery of marriage is that oneness involves more than physical unity. True, in God's eyes, a unique unity takes place when a man and woman join in sexual relationship, whether it be a permanent or a promiscuous relationship (see 1 Cor. 6:15,16). But God's perfect will is that it be a permanent relationship, involving one man and one woman, reflecting the original creation. This is also why Jesus said to the religious philosophers of His day, "What therefore God has joined together, let no man separate" (Matt. 19:6).

It is also true that sexual intercourse was designed by God to be simply the beginning of a growing oneness and unity in marriage—a unity and oneness that is far more than physical.

Perhaps this can best be illustrated with the way the Bible describes Christian conversion. A person becomes a Christian by placing his faith in Jesus Christ for personal salvation. At that moment, he becomes one with Christ. In this sense, each of us individually, and all Christians collectively, are "married" to Christ. Obviously, this is figurative language, but it is the very picture Paul painted in his Ephesian letter when discussing the relationship that exists between a husband and wife (see Eph. 5:22,23,32), as well as between Christ and His followers.

However, becoming one with Christ at conversion—when we personally receive Christ as Savior (see John 1:12)—does not mean that our unity with Christ is experientially complete. It is true that God views us as one with Christ the moment we become true believers. But to experience that unity in all of its fullness is yet another matter. As long as Christians are on earth, we have the potential to grow in our relationship with Jesus Christ, both personally and corporately. The Bible teaches that someday we will be one with Him in heaven; the process will then be complete. In the book of Revelation, this ultimate experience is called the "marriage supper."

To a certain extent, this process should also be true in a literal marriage, although this human relationship, according to Jesus, will terminate once we leave this earth. We will no longer need this kind of human relationship to be fulfilled and happy. Jesus Christ will be all we need. But, while on earth, our spiritual relationship with Christ illustrates our relationship with our marital partner. The act of sexual intercourse, in God's eyes, indeed makes a man and woman one flesh. But it is designed to be only a beginning point in a great adventure in getting to know each other, not only physically but psychologically and spiritually. True experiential unity and oneness are yet future for a newly married couple. Like our total relationship with Christ, our total relationship with our marital partner must be carefully nurtured and developed. Only then will we begin to experience true oneness.

An Exercise in Becoming One

In God's sight, when a man and woman are joined in a sexual union, they become one, whether or not it is personally or mutually satisfying. But marital unity that is total—physical, psychological and spiritual—involves a process that takes time, insight, sensitivity and effort. Furthermore, it is in this larger context of unity that sexual oneness, which is mutually satisfying, also takes place. Without this broader setting, even sexual satisfaction can become rather meaningless and even boring. All the sexual techniques in the world, without developing total unity, can leave a marriage in shambles. This is one reason why the divorce rate is increasing in our society at a time when we've known more about male and female sexuality than at any other moment in history.

Because it is true that total unity is God's plan for a man and woman, the major part of this study together is designed to help you, as a couple, develop this total unity in marriage. So, let's get started!

Plan a Time
As a couple, spend a few minutes discussing with each other a time when you can get together each week to work through this material. Find a place where you will be uninterrupted for a couple of hours.

For example, when we, as a couple, first worked through this process, we found a quiet place in a local park. Weather permitting, we met together, seated at a picnic table, working through personal projects.

Sign a Contract
The following is a simple contract. As a couple, sign it, agreeing to commit yourself to work through the projects together in this book. Though it may appear an unnecessary request, a contractual commitment of this nature is very helpful when the pressures of other things threaten to sidetrack us from our initial commitments.

As a couple, and with God's help, we covenant together to complete the assignments in this study entitled *Partners for Life.*

Signed _____

Signed _____

Date _____

Step 1: Instructions for Both Spouses

Take as much time as necessary to record the answers to the following exercises. Be as specific as possible. Do *not* discuss the answers with your husband/wife until you read the instructions following this step in the assignment.

Step 1—An Exercise for Wives

1. If you could point out three things about your husband
   that please you most, what would they be? Why?
   Three things about my husband that please me the
   most:

   a.

   b.

   c.

   The reasons why these three things please me:

   a.

   b.

   c.

2. What would you say are your husband's three greatest strengths? Explain why you think these are his
   greatest strengths. Three of my husband's greatest
   strengths:

   a.

   b.

   c.

(over)

Three reasons why I believe these are my husband's greatest strengths:

    a.

    b.

    c.

3. List one way in which your husband could help you become a more fulfilled person.

4. What one thing in your husband's personality or behavioral patterns causes you the most stress? Explain.

5. If you could change one thing about your husband, what would it be?

Step 1—An Exercise for Husbands

1. If you could point out three things about your wife that please you most, what would they be? Why? Three things about my wife that please me the most:

   a.

   b.

   c.

   The reasons why these three things please me:

   a.

   b

   c

2. What would you say are your wife's three greatest strengths? Explain why you think these are her greatest strengths. Three of my wife's greatest strengths:

   a.

   b.

   c.

(over)

Three reasons why I believe these are my wife's greatest strengths:

    a.

    b.

    c.

3. List one way in which your wife could help you become a more fulfilled person.

4. What one thing in your wife's personality or behavioral patterns causes you the most stress? Explain.

5. If you could change one thing about your wife, what would it be?

Step 2: Instructions for Both Spouses

Now that you have completed this first assignment, share your responses with each other. Flip a coin to see who goes first and then share the answers to item 1. Then move on to the second item. For example, if the husband goes first, he would share the responses to item 1. The wife would then share her responses to item 1. Then move on to item 2, item 3, etc., taking turns until you have completed all five items.

Note: It is important that you do not discuss the answers to these questions the first time through. Just listen to each other share responses. Both of you need time to reflect and develop objectivity. It is very important that you do not respond, even though you may want to—especially in a negative sense. Attempt to avoid even nonverbal reactions, such as looking away in disgust, or just looking away.

If you're really going to listen to your husband or wife, you must *really* listen—nondefensively, intently, objectively and with feeling. You must not even allow yourself to think about how you are going to answer or respond. You will have plenty of time after you have listened to decide what you are going to say. In fact, if you are really listening, you will be able to formulate your response more adequately after you've listened.

Alternate Suggestion: If you have difficulty communicating out loud as you're working through this exercise, you may simply need to let your mate read your answers. Furthermore, if you become emotionally involved and want to defend yourself in response to your mate's comments, determine that you will wait a couple of days before continuing to discuss your responses. Becoming negative during this first assignment causes some marital partners to give up immediately and not to proceed with this study together. Avoid this at all costs.

Additional Suggestion: If what your mate is saying is too painful to handle, simply extend your open hand in a "please stop" position indicating you cannot bear to hear more at this moment. With this nonverbal gesture, you are simply asking for time to build up your emotional tolerance, particularly to avoid a negative reaction. You may need to wait until another time to regain your composure. As marital partners, respect and honor this request without indicating you feel it is a weakness. However, if you use this method, try never to use it as a cop-out or escape from facing reality. If you do, you will never grow together as you should in your marriage.

Note: If you cannot work through the answers to these items by following the above suggestions, you are definitely in need of marital counseling. You are having serious difficulty communicating in your marriage. You need an objective third party to help you listen to each other. This may be your pastor, a respected Bible study leader or a professional counselor. By all means, do not let pride and fear stand in your way of overcoming this hurdle.

Step 3: Instructions for Both Spouses

Now that you have shared your thoughts with each other without verbal reactions, go back and respond to each other's answers. Go through each item again, alternating as before, asking your marital partner for more clarification and elaboration. Be positive. Ask your partner to explain these comments. Try to hear as much as you can so as to know how your mate really thinks and feels.

Note: If one or the other of you is not understanding clearly, there will be plenty of opportunity in the following exercises to get more insight and to state your own opinions. In fact, if you learn to listen to each other without reacting emotionally, changes will begin to take place in your own perceptions of each other as you go through the following exercises.

Step 4: Instructions for Both Spouses

Review the time and place you will meet to complete the next section in this study together. If comfortable, close in prayer and thank the Lord for the opportunity to listen to each other and to grow together in your marriage. Before you pray, you may wish to use Paul's statement to the Philippians, which we have adapted slightly to apply to marriage:

> *I thank my God every time I remember you. In all my prayers for you, I always pray with joy because of your partnership from the first day until now, being confident of this, that He who began a good work in you will carry it on to completion until the day of Christ Jesus* (see Phil. 1:3-6).

Notes
1. Allan Bloom, *The Closing of the American Mind* (New York: Simon & Schuster, 1987), p. 119.
2. All italicized words in scriptural statements used in this book are the author's and are used to emphasize and clarify certain ideas and concepts.
3. F. Foulkes, *The Epistle of Paul to the Ephesians* (Grand Rapids: Wm. B. Eerdmans Publishing Company, 1963), p. 161.
4. C. F. Keil and F. Delitzsch, *The Pentateuch* (Grand Rapids: Wm. B. Eerdmans Publishing Company, No Date), p. 86.

2

BREAKING FAMILY TIES

The biblical statement about marriage, which we looked at in the first chapter, contains another very significant principle for growing together in your marriage. Not only do a man and woman who come together in marriage become one flesh with unbounding potential for experiential unity and oneness, but the Word of God also says: "For this cause a man [and woman] *shall leave his father and mother*" (Eph. 5:31).

In the most literal sense, the Bible is simply referring to leaving certain established relationships with one family and starting another. It is only logical that a man and woman cannot become truly one in a practical sense unless they break certain ties with their parents and establish their own enduring relationship.

But this statement has profound implications beyond just literal separation. In fact, it may be true that the real meaning is more related to emotional than physical separation. The fact is that children in biblical settings who separated from their parents did not necessarily move away from their parents. In their culture, they often lived under the same roof or right next door. The extended family was a part of their societal structures.

But it is also true that geographical proximity often makes it more difficult to leave father and mother in the true and most profound sense of what that means. In some respects, we have some cultural advantages over those who lived in the Old Testament and New Testament setting. Nevertheless, it is still difficult for most of us to handle the emotional ties with our parents and to develop our own personal and marital identities. The following are some typical illustrations of what may happen.

Developing Unhealthy Dependence

Bill and Mary are newly-married. Because Mary's parents have a large home and because the newlyweds are trying to finish college, Mary's parents have invited Bill and Mary to live with them.

Is this wrong? Not necessarily. However, there's a problem. Bill, like most young men who marry early, has certain vulnerabilities. He knows Mary's parents are relatively well-to-do and are very unselfish with their material possessions. Consequently, under the financial pressures and demands of college, Bill is becoming more and more dependent on his wife's parents to meet his and Mary's material needs. Since he has not had to face the realities of life and his own responsibilities to support and care for Mary, he is not growing and maturing in this aspect of his life.

Will this turn out bad? Again, not necessarily. But the situation has certain potential dangers that could eventually blow the lid off this new marriage.

For example, because of Bill's attitudes and behavior,

Mary could be developing resentful feelings toward her husband, which could eventually erupt. Or, she could continue to harbor these feelings, never expressing them, and go into a state of depression.

Bill could also develop some very bad habit patterns, both emotionally and volitionally. Life is filled with threatening responsibilities, and having to face them for the first time later in life doesn't make it easier. But the temptation is always there to rely on good old Dad and Mom to help out in financial binds.

Then, too, living with parents who are well-to-do makes it emotionally difficult for newly-married couples to eventually live in a small, sparsely furnished apartment that is commensurate with their income. For most young couples starting out, it will take a number of years—as it often did for their parents—to have sufficient resources to live more comfortably.

The principle of leaving father and mother is a valid one, and both parents and children should face the issue immediately, making whatever adjustments are necessary.

On the other hand, this does not mean that parents who are able should not be considerate of their married children and help them meet their needs. But should their help become a stumbling block in their children's marital adjustments, they must face this problem head-on. The most loving thing parents can do is to adjust their behavior so as to help both children leave father and mother and establish their own home, responsibly and successfully. Furthermore, a young couple who sees a dependency syndrome developing should initiate the break themselves if their parents do not, regardless of how extremely painful it may be at the time. Ultimate happiness is far more important than immediate comfort.

Immature Parents

There's another side to this problem. Sometimes proximity brings out the immaturity in parents rather than in their children. For example, Tom and Jane are living next door to Tom's parents. Tom is an only son and, though his mother loves Jane, down deep she has never felt there would ever be a girl quite good enough for her son (a rather common emotion for most mothers). Try as she might to overcome these feelings, she struggles with them every day. Unfortunately, living so closely together

---

Most of us have emotional "spillovers" from our home life that transfer to our mates and make it difficult to truly leave father and mother.

---

emphasizes Jane's inadequacies as a young bride and homemaker, which, in turn, accentuates her mother-in-law's emotional problem.

Try as she might, Tom's mother can't cover up her feelings. Jane is threatened by it all. Furthermore, Tom, as a young husband who also loves his mother, is slowly becoming convinced, through his mother's subtle innuendos, that maybe Jane was a poor choice after all. For one thing, Tom can't quite seem to understand why his young working wife can't keep up the home the same way as his older, nonworking mother.

Obviously, this marriage is headed for serious problems because of constant closeness. But again, all of us can point to children who *do* live next door or in the same house with their parents for a while with very few, if any, problems. But the principle of leaving father and mother is a valid one, and both parents and children should face the issue immediately, making whatever adjustments are necessary.

Generally, it is advisable in our culture to establish a

certain degree of physical and geographical separation in order to avoid any potential problems. Because of the very nature of life, most of us—both parents and children—have a sufficient number of hang-ups to make us vulnerable. At this point, an old adage is very appropriate: *An ounce of prevention is worth a pound of cure.*

Emotions and Transference

When speaking of hang-ups, it's important to realize that most of us have emotional "spillovers" from our home life that transfer to our mates and make it difficult to truly leave father and mother. In fact, the phenomenon is inevitable, regardless of how ideal our childhood experiences. All mothers and wives and fathers and husbands have many things in common.

Let me illustrate. Before he married, John's mother washed his clothes, made his bed, cooked his meals, and kept up the house. Now he's married and his wife, Sally, washes his clothes, makes his bed, cooks his meals and keeps up the house. Though Sally is involved in performing the same functions John's mother once did, she does things differently. For one thing, she's not quite as efficient. She doesn't organize his socks the way his mother did, and sometimes she doesn't have the bed made when he gets home from work. And her meal schedule is not as regular. These similar functions, combined with the dissimilar procedures, irritate John to no end. He finds himself reacting emotionally to Sally, and constantly compares her openly with his mother. This, of course, makes Sally furious. In fact, it makes her want to do just the opposite from John's mother.

Sally's problems are also aggravated by the fact that her husband, John, reminds her of her father, who was always picking on her mother, putting her on a performance standard and reminding her that she did not measure up to his own mother.

This process is often, at least partially, subconscious. There are times when things we don't really understand about our mates irritate us. Subconsciously, over the years, we have repressed certain feelings and emotions we had toward our parents. Unknown to us, we subtly transfer these covert emotions to a husband or wife. This can happen even though we have been reared in a relatively happy home situation.

I [Gene] remember this process at work in my own life. After I was married, I experienced certain spontaneous negative feelings toward Elaine when she would ask me to do certain things—particularly if she expressed her desires with a certain tone of voice. It wasn't until years later, while visiting my parents' home, that I began to see the connection. I found myself—during that visit—reacting to my mother emotionally just as I had been reacting to my wife. I had come full circle. Old emotional memories suddenly came to the surface. I clearly saw the source of my more recent emotional feelings and reactions toward my wife. They had been there all along at a subconscious level. In reality, when I reacted to my wife's requests, I was reacting to my mother. Those reactions did not necessarily relate to whether or not I loved or respected my mother, which I did and still do. They were natural feelings I had not understood or dealt with properly as I was growing up.

I [Elaine] also remember this process at work in my own life. After we were married, I experienced certain negative reactions when Gene expressed any kind of physical affection in front of the children. I'm not referring to inappropriate affection—but rather natural and normal expressions.

Eventually I came to understand the source of these reactions. I remember, as a little girl, seeing my mother, on a number of occasions, push my father away anytime he tried to show affection to her. I understand now that part of her reactions were cultural and part of them related to some struggles my father and mother were having at that point in their own marital relationship. Years later, my mother's model became, in a real sense, an influence in developing my own reactions to my own husband in my own marriage. Understanding these dynamics freed me not only to want physical affection from Gene in the presence of the children, but to express it as well. In fact, my own children grew up not even realizing that I had these internal struggles at one point in our marriage. Though I had the negative feelings, I never allowed them to override what I knew was a proper response. However, understanding these dynamics did indeed free me up in this area of what God intended to be a normal and natural response, both emotionally and physically.

An Exercise in Leaving Parents

The following exercises are designed to help you understand the emotional dynamics involved in your own marriage. They will help you determine the extent to which you have actually left your father and mother psychologically. Analyzing your responses will help you isolate problems in this area of your marriage and then help you begin to resolve them. Personal insight is absolutely essential in properly breaking family ties, and these exercises are designed to help you gain that insight, as well as set specific goals that are necessary.

Step 1: Instructions for Both Spouses

Circle the number that best describes your personal situation. *Note*: Your initial mental and emotional responses to the following statements and to the answers on the scale are probably your most valid responses.

Step 1—An Exercise for Wives

Dependence v. Independence

	Never	Seldom	Sometimes	Frequently
1. When I feel insecurity, I have a strong desire to share it with my mother.	1	2	3	4
2. When I get angry at my husband, I have a strong desire to tell my mother.	1	2	3	4
3. When I get lonesome, I have a strong desire to visit my mother.	1	2	3	4
4. When my mate misunderstands me, I have a strong desire to talk with my mother.	1	2	3	4
5. When I have problems with my children, I have a strong desire to seek my mother's advice.	1	2	3	4
6. When we run out of money, I have a strong desire to ask my mother for financial help.	1	2	3	4
7. When I feel insecurity, I have a strong desire to share it with my father.	1	2	3	4
8. When I get angry at my husband, I have a strong desire to visit with my father.	1	2	3	4
9. When I get lonesome, I have a strong desire to visit with my father.	1	2	3	4
10. When my mate misunderstands me, I have a strong desire to talk with my father.	1	2	3	4
11. When I have problems with my children, I have a strong desire to seek my father's advice.	1	2	3	4
12. When we run short of money, I have a strong desire to ask my father for financial help.	1	2	3	4

(over)

Step 2:

Now that you have completed the "Dependence v. Independence" scales, study your answers on the scales you just completed and take the time you need to answer the following questions. Note that number 1's indicating "never" and number 4's indicating "frequently" are the most significant responses to look at. Numbers 2 and 3 indicating "seldom" and "sometimes" are very normal and natural responses. In some instances, however, the numbers 1 and 4 may also be normal and natural. You'll need to make that judgment in view of your overall responses.

Write your answers to the following:

1. As a wife, list the areas where you are overly dependent on your mother.

2. Also list the areas where you are overly independent.

3. As a wife, list any areas where you are overly dependent on your father.

4. Also list the areas where you are overly independent.

5. How do the areas you've listed above affect your marital relationship? Be specific.

An Exercise for Wives

Mature or Immature Parents

Circle the number that best describes your personal situation.

	Never	Seldom	Sometimes	Frequently
1. My mother communicates with me to see how I'm doing in our marriage.	1	2	3	4
2. My mother criticizes my mate.	1	2	3	4
3. My mother sends me money.	1	2	3	4
4. My mother criticizes me.	1	2	3	4
5. My mother is upset if I don't contact her regularly.	1	2	3	4
6. My mother is quite disturbed if we visit my husband's parents more often than we visit my parents.	1	2	3	4
7. My father communicates with me to see how I'm doing in my marriage.	1	2	3	4
8. My father criticizes my husband.	1	2	3	4
9. My father sends me money.	1	2	3	4
10. My father criticizes me.	1	2	3	4
11. My father is upset if I don't contact him regularly.	1	2	3	4
12. My father is quite disturbed if we visit my husband's parents more often than we visit my parents.	1	2	3	4

(over)

Parental Maturity

1. List the areas of maturity you can identify in your parents.

2. List the areas of immaturity.

3. How do these areas of maturity and/or immaturity affect your relationship with your husband?

An Exercise for Wives

Emotional Transference

Circle the number that best describes your personal situation.

	Never	Seldom	Sometimes	Frequently
1. When my husband asks me to wash his clothes, I experience negative feelings.	1	2	3	4
2. When my husband asks me to sew a button on his clothes, I feel negative feelings.	1	2	3	4
3. When my husband asks me to fix a meal, I experience negative feelings.	1	2	3	4
4. When my husband asks me to make love, I experience negative feelings.	1	2	3	4
5. When my husband asks me to overcome a habit, I experience negative feelings.	1	2	3	4
6. When my husband asks me to help him with his work, I experience negative feelings.	1	2	3	4
7. When my husband asks me to run an errand, I experience negative feelings.	1	2	3	4
8. When my husband asks me to keep a certain time schedule, I experience negative feelings.	1	2	3	4
9. When my husband disagrees with me, I get angry.	1	2	3	4
10. When my husband makes a suggestion to me, I get emotionally upset.	1	2	3	4

(over)

Write your answers to the following:

1. List any negative emotions you've experienced toward your parents that you are now transferring to your husband.

2. How does this affect your husband's attitude and behavior toward you?

Step 1—An Exercise for Husbands

Dependence vs. Independence

	Never	Seldom	Sometimes	Frequently
1. When I feel insecurity, I have a strong desire to share it with my mother.	1	2	3	4
2. When I get angry at my wife, I have a strong desire to tell my mother.	1	2	3	4
3. When I get lonesome, I have a strong desire to visit my mother.	1	2	3	4
4. When my mate misunderstands me, I have a strong desire to talk to my mother.	1	2	3	4
5. When I have problems with my children, I have a strong desire to seek my mother's advice.	1	2	3	4
6. When we run out of money, I have a strong desire to ask my mother for financial help.	1	2	3	4
7. When I feel insecurity, I have a strong desire to share it with my father.	1	2	3	4
8. When I get angry at my wife, I have a strong desire to visit with my father.	1	2	3	4
9. When I get lonesome, I have a strong desire to visit with my father.	1	2	3	4
10. When my mate misunderstands me, I have a strong desire to talk with my father.	1	2	3	4
11. When I have problems with my children, I have a strong desire to seek my father's advice.	1	2	3	4
12. When we run short of money, I have a strong desire to ask my father for financial help.	1	2	3	4

(over)

Step 2:

Now that you have completed the "Dependence v. Independence" scales, study your answers on the scales you just completed and take the time you need to answer the following questions. Note that number 1's indicating "never" and number 4's indicating "frequently" are the most significant responses to look at. Numbers 2 and 3 indicating "seldom" and "sometimes" are very normal and natural responses. In some instances, however, the numbers 1 and 4 may also be normal and natural. You'll need to make that judgment in view of your overall responses.

Write your answers to the following:

1. As a husband, list the areas where you are overly dependent on your mother.

2. Also list the areas where you are overly independent.

3. As a husband, list any areas where you are overly dependent on your father.

4. Also list the areas where you are overly independent.

5. How do the areas you've listed above affect your marital relationship? Be specific.

An Exercise for Husbands

Mature or Immature Parents

Circle the number that best describes your personal situation.

	Never	Seldom	Sometimes	Frequently
1. My mother communicates with me to see how I'm doing in our marriage.	1	2	3	4
2. My mother criticizes my mate.	1	2	3	4
3. My mother sends me money.	1	2	3	4
4. My mother criticizes me.	1	2	3	4
5. My mother is upset if I don't contact her regularly.	1	2	3	4
6. My mother is quite disturbed if we visit my wife's parents more often than we visit my parents.	1	2	3	4
7. My father communicates with me to see how I'm doing in my marriage.	1	2	3	4
8. My father criticizes my wife.	1	2	3	4
9. My father sends me money.	1	2	3	4
10. My father criticizes me.	1	2	3	4
11. My father is upset if I don't contact him regularly.	1	2	3	4
12. My father is quite disturbed if we visit my wife's parents more often than we visit my parents.	1	2	3	4

(over)

Parental Maturity

1. List the areas of maturity you can identify in your parents.

2. List the areas of immaturity.

3. How do these areas of maturity and/or immaturity affect your relationship with your wife?

An Exercise for Husbands

Emotional Transference

Circle the number that best describes your personal situation.

	Never	Seldom	Sometimes	Frequently
1. When my wife asks me to help with the dishes, I experience negative feelings.	1	2	3	4
2. When my wife asks me to carry out the garbage, I experience negative feelings.	1	2	3	4
3. When my wife asks me to help with the housework, I experience negative feelings.	1	2	3	4
4. When my wife asks me to show affection, I experience negative feelings.	1	2	3	4
5. When my wife asks me to overcome a habit, I experience negative feelings.	1	2	3	4
6. When my wife asks me to watch the children, I experience negative feelings.	1	2	3	4
7. When my wife asks me to account for money I spend, I experience negative feelings.	1	2	3	4
8. When my wife asks me to keep a certain time schedule, I experience negative feelings.	1	2	3	4
9. When my wife disagrees with me, I get angry.	1	2	3	4
10. When my wife makes a suggestion to me, I get emotionally upset.	1	2	3	4

(over)

Write your answers to the following:

1. List any negative emotions you've experienced toward your parents that you are now transferring to your wife.

2. How does this affect your wife's attitude and behavior toward you?

Step 3—Setting Goals: Instructions for Both Spouses

Isolating problems and understanding their nature is the place to start in reaching concrete solutions. However, we must go a step further. Insight is only the beginning. We must set specific goals to overcome these problems. What goals should you set in your marriage in order to help you truly leave father and mother? The following illustrations will help you in your goal- setting process:

Case 1:
Jane has a consistent tendency to talk to her mother every time she feels insecurity in her marriage. Her goal is to share sensitively these feelings with her husband rather than her mother. Jim, her husband, has set up the goal to listen objectively and nondefensively to Jane when she shares these feelings and to do what he can to help her overcome her insecurities.

Case 2:
Jim reacts negatively to his wife every time she asks him to do something around the house. His primary goal is to volunteer to do certain things before he is asked. Secondly, his goal is to be emotionally open to his wife's requests—realizing he is subconsciously reacting to his mother. On the other hand, Jane's goal is to ask Jim to do things with a different tone of voice. She realizes she conveys her desires in a rather demanding way. So, she is trying to avoid sounding like Jim's mother.

Case 3:
Both Jim and Jane realize that his mother tries to control their marriage. They have set up two short-range goals and one long-range goal.

First, Jim is going to talk to his mother openly but sensitively, asking her not to interfere with his marriage. He plans to talk with his father privately, explaining why he is going to talk with his mother.

Second, Jane is simultaneously going to do all she can to let Jim's mother know she really cares about her—sending her notes of appreciation, calling her periodically to carry on a friendly conversation, etc.

Third, if the problem persists, Jim and Jane are considering moving to another part of the city to avoid geographical closeness.

Step 3—My Goals as a Wife

In order to more adequately carry out the biblical injunction to leave father and mother, I am, as a wife, setting up the following goals in my relationship with my husband.

Note: In writing your goals, use actions words to describe specific behavior. For example, you might write:

"I will sensitively share . . . . "
"I will listen objectively and nondefensively . . . . "
"I will volunteer to . . . . "
"I will be emotionally open . . . . "
"I will use a different tone of voice when . . . . "
"I will write a note of appreciation . . . . "

1. I will . . . .

2. I will . . . .

3. I will . . . .

Step 3—My Goals as a Husband

In order to more adequately carry out the biblical injunction to leave father and mother, I am, as a husband, setting up the following goals in my relationship with my wife.

Note: In writing your goals, use actions words to describe specific behavior. For example, you might write:

"I will sensitively share . . . . "
"I will listen objectively and nondefensively . . . . "
"I will volunteer to . . . . "
"I will be emotionally open . . . . "
"I will use a different tone of voice when . . . . "
"I will write a note of appreciation . . . . "

1.   I will . . . .

2.   I will . . . .

3.   I will . . . .

Step 4—Instructions for Both Spouses

Now that you have written out specific goals, share them with each other. Discuss how you can help each other achieve your specific goals.

Close your time together in prayer. You may wish to use Paul's prayer for the Ephesians, applying what he says to the experience that you've just had:

> *For this reason, ever since I heard about your faith in the Lord Jesus and your love for all the saints, I have not stopped giving thanks for you, remembering you in my prayers. I keep asking that the God of our Lord Jesus Christ, the glorious Father, may give you the Spirit of wisdom and revelation, so that you may know him better. I pray also that the eyes of your heart may be enlightened in order that you may know the hope to which he has called you, the riches of his glorious inheritance in the saints, and his incomparably great power for us who believe* (Eph. 1:15-19, *NIV*).

3
LOVING AS CHRIST LOVED

In this chapter and the next, we want to look at two important directives to husbands and wives that we believe have frequently been misinterpreted. In his letter to the Ephesians, Paul exhorted husbands to *love their wives "as Christ loved the church and gave himself up for her"* (Eph. 5:25, *NIV*). He also exhorted wives to *submit to their husbands "as to the Lord"* (Eph. 5:22, *NIV*).

Directives to All Christians

"Loving as Christ loved" is not an exclusive directive for husbands. Nor is "submitting" an exclusive directive for wives. At the beginning of chapter 5, before directing his thoughts specifically to husbands, Paul had already addressed all Christians and exhorted them to *"live a life of love*, just as Christ loved us and gave himself up for us"* (Eph. 5:2, *NIV*).   And immediately preceding his directive to wives to submit to their husbands as to the Lord, he had instructed all believers to *"submit to one* another out of reverence for Christ" (Eph. 5:21, *NIV*). In other words, all Christians are to love one another following Christ's model, and all believers are to mutually submit to one another.

Special Directives to Husbands and Wives

Why, then, did Paul exhort husbands to love as Christ loved when he had already instructed all Christians to do the same? And why did he exhort wives to submit to their husbands when he had already instructed all Christians to submit to one another? We believe the answer is found in Genesis 3:16. When Adam and Eve disobeyed God, they not only plunged the whole world into sin, but they also created some unique problems for husbands and wives. Though God's thoughts are directed toward Eve in this verse, what he said focused on what would be enduring weaknesses in both wives and husbands. First, "Your *desire* shall be for your husband," he told Eve. And, second, Adam "shall rule over you."

All Christians are to love one another following Christ's model, and all believers are to mutually submit to one another.

With this first statement, Paul was telling Eve and all wives thereafter that they would have a strong desire and natural tendency to want to usurp the authority of their husbands—in short, to be unsubmissive. And husbands, God said, would have a natural tendency to dominate, control and rule over their wives.[1]

Even a superficial study of world history, as well as a bit of honest introspection by all husbands and wives, will reveal that this is exactly what has happened. Though affected and modified to a certain degree by various cultural situations, these natural tendencies have been there in every society since the dawn of creation and have been either covertly or overtly expressed. Because of man's tendency toward domination, women have often been forced to achieve their goals in more subtle ways. In fact, the most cunning have actually deceived their husbands into thinking they (the husbands) are in control while, in reality, the wives are wielding tremendous power, particularly by utilizing sex as their weapon. Men, on the other hand, have been far from subtle. History, generally, is basically the story of men blatantly using women for their own selfish pleasure.

Paul's concern, then, in his letter to the Ephesians (see also Col.3:18,19), focuses on this age old problem. Though all of us, because of the sin of Adam and Eve, tend to be both unsubmissive and unloving in our relationships with others, the natural tendencies stated by God in the Garden of Eden continue to plague husbands and wives in a unique way to this very day. Furthermore, coming to know Christ personally and experiencing God's saving grace does not eliminate this tendency. If it did, Paul would not have instructed those first century Christian husbands to "love their wives just as Christ loved the church." Nor would he have had to exhort those Christian wives to "submit to their husbands as to the Lord."

Loving as Christ Loved

Having made these distinctions and having, hopefully, clarified why Paul zeros in on "loving" for husbands and "submitting" for wives, let's move back to the larger context in Paul's letter to the Ephesians. He wrote:

> *Be imitators of God, therefore, as dearly loved*
> *children and live a life of love, just as Christ*

loved us and gave himself up for us as a fragrant offering and sacrifice to God (Eph. 5:1,2,
NIV).

What does it mean to love "as Christ loved"? Perhaps
the most graphic illustration is given by Paul in his letter
to the Philippians. Initially, Paul gave a specific exhorta-
tion: "Do *nothing* out of selfish ambition or vain conceit,
but in humility consider others better than yourselves.
Each of you should look not only to your own interests,
but also to the interests of others" (Phil. 2:3,4, *NIV*).

---

*The principle of loving as Christ loved puts the focus
primarily on our partner's needs, not on our own.*

Just reading this paragraph from Paul's letter makes
it quite clear how this directive will affect a marital relationship. The principle of loving as Christ loved puts the
focus primarily on our partner's needs, not on our own. In
everything we do, our goal should be to consider the
other person's needs and concerns first.

Paul goes on to spell out how Christ demonstrated
these attitudes and actions toward us.

*First, he said, there's to be an attitude of unselfish-
ness.* "Your attitude should be the same as that of Christ
Jesus: Who, being in very nature God, did not consider
equality with God something to be grasped" (Phil. 2:5,6,
NIV).

In other words, Christ did not cling to His heavenly
position with His Father, but was willing to lay it aside to
come into this world—the world He had made. And, in
His incarnation, He identified with our fallen condition,
though He, of course, did not personally participate in
sin. He did, however, give up the glories of heaven to live
among men. And, when He did so, He was demonstrat-

ing an unselfish attitude that is unparalleled in the universe.

Second, Christ's love was demonstrated by an attitude of humility (see Phil. 2:7). Christ, who was "in very nature God" (v. 6), voluntarily "made himself nothing." He who created all things temporarily laid aside His heavenly glory. He who was and is God took upon Himself "the very nature of a servant." He who made man took upon Himself "human likeness." This, of course, is ultimate humility personified.

Third, Christ demonstrated an attitude of sacrifice and self-giving. His actions illustrate the greatest act of love ever known to mankind. "Being found in appearance as a man, he humbled himself and became obedient to death—even death on a cross!" (Phil. 2:8, *NIV*). Jesus Christ died that we might live eternally. Because man's sin demanded the penalty of death, Jesus Christ died for every human being, even His enemies. Thus, when they nailed Him to the cross, He prayed, "Father, forgive them, for they do not know what they are doing" (Luke 23:34, *NIV*).

Paul wrote these words in Philippians to all Christians, who are supposed to emulate Christ in their relationships with others. But it is also a powerful demonstration and elaboration for both husbands and wives of what it means to love as Christ loved.

An Exercise in True Loving

To love as Christ loved is probably one of the most difficult challenges facing any couple. It calls for attitudes
and actions that run contrary to our natural inclinations. It
is much easier for most of us to receive than to give; to
be self-centered than to focus on others; to be ministered
unto than to minister. And, indeed, we must be able to
receive, to have our share of attention and to be ministered unto. But to focus on ourselves primarily destroys
that unique process that must put others first if we are to
follow Christ's example. The following exercise will help
you develop these qualities in your own life first—and
then in your marriage.

Step 1—Instructions for Both Spouses

As a husband and wife, complete the following evaluation scales designed for each of you.

Step 1—Scale 1 for Wives

Evaluate your relationship with your husband in light of Christ's examples of unselfishness, humility, sacrifice and self-giving. The following evaluation scales will assist you in this process. If the statement is *mostly true,* circle the "T." If the statement is *mostly false,* circle the "F." *Note:* Some of the following statements may not be applicable to your situation. If so, simply mark them with an "F" (false).

__ 1. When my husband comes home   T   F
from work, I immediately ask him to
sit down and listen to my problems.

__ 2. When I see my husband has a few   T   F
spare moments at home, I present
him with a list of things that I want him
to do around the house.

__ 3. I resent it when my husband sits   T   F
down in the family room and watches
television—especially when I'm preparing a meal.

__ 4. I expect my husband to take care of   T   F
the children while he's home.

__ 5. I resent the fact that my husband is   T   F
away from the children during the
day and I have to take care of them.

__ 6. I find myself quite frequently emo-   T   F
tionally resistant when I know my
husband has sexual interests and
needs.

__ 7. I resent the fact that my husband   T   F
gets more attention from others than I
do.

__ 8. I resent having to cook meals and   T   F
take care of the home.

__ 9. I want to eat out most of the time.   T   F

(over)

___10. I sleep late most days, getting up after my husband leaves for work.   T   F

___11. I usually stay up late to do things after my husband goes to bed.   T   F

___12. I seldom ask my husband what I can do to help him with his work.   T   F

___13. I spend more time with my friends than with my husband.   T   F

___14. When I have a choice between setting aside time to be with my husband or my friends, I usually set aside time to be with my friends.   T   F

___15. When I have a choice between setting aside time to be with my husband or my children, I usually set aside time to be with my children.   T   F

___16. I seldom call my husband at work and tell him I miss him and love him.   T   F

___17. I seldom plan how I can make my husband feel welcome when he comes home.   T   F

___18. I seldom think about my husband's personal needs.   T   F

___19. I seldom think about how to be a creative lover.   T   F

___20. I seldom initiate sexual relations.   T   F

___21. I seldom think about my husband during the day.   T   F

___22. I seldom make an effort to know what my husband is doing during the day—that is, his personal work schedule.   T   F

___23. I'd rather spend most of my time by myself.   T   F

___24. When I know I'm going to be gone when my husband comes home, I usually do not leave a note of expla-

(continued)

nation or call him and explain changes in my personal scheduling.

___25. I seldom seek my husband's consent to do things.   T   F

___26. I resent the fact that I don't have a separate bank account.   T   F

___27. If I had to do it over again, I'd rather not have children.   T   F

___28. I seldom thank my husband for his commitment to his job and providing materially for my personal needs.   T   F

___29. I resent having to care for children, keep up the home, prepare meals, etc.   T   F

___30. I resent my husband's sexual requests.   T   F

___31. I resent the fact that my husband is fulfilled sexually.   T   F

___32. I seldom write love notes to my husband.   T   F

___33. I seldom tell my husband how much I love him.   T   F

___34. I resent the children's demands upon my husband when I want to spend time with him privately.   T   F

Step 1—Scale 1 for Husbands

Evaluate your relationship with your wife in light of Christ's examples of unselfishness, humility, sacrifice and self-giving. The following evaluation scales will assist you in this process. If the statement is *mostly true,* circle the "T." If the statement is *mostly false,* circle the "F." *Note:* Some of the following statements may not be applicable to your situation. If so, simply mark these with an "F" (false).

___ 1. When I come home from work, I immediately seek a place of privacy where I can do my own thing.   T   F

___ 2. When I come home from work, I want my wife to be available immediately to listen to my problems.   T   F

___ 3. I resent it when my wife is running behind in meal preparation.   T   F

___ 4. I do not expect to help with the children when I'm home.   T   F

___ 5. I seldom think about the burden my wife carries when she is home with the children.   T   F

___ 6. When I want to have sexual relations with my wife, I seldom think about her personal schedule.   T   F

___ 7. I resent it when my wife gets attention.   T   F

___ 8. I seldom thank my wife for cooking meals and taking care of the home.   T   F

___ 9. I seldom suggest to my wife that we eat out.   T   F

___10. I resent it when my wife sleeps late in the morning.   T   F

___11. I resent it when my wife stays up late to get things done around the house.   T   F

(over)

__12. I seldom ask my wife what I can do to   T   F
help her with her work.

__13. When I have a day off, I usually plan   T   F
to spend it with my male companions
(golfing, playing tennis, etc.).

__14. When I have a choice between   T   F
spending time with my wife or my
friends, I usually choose to spend
time with my friends.

__15. When I have a choice between   T   F
spending time with my wife or my
children, I usually choose to spend
time with my children.

__16. I seldom call my wife during the day   T   F
and tell her I miss her and love her.

__17. I seldom think about how I can   T   F
encourage my wife when I come
home from work.

__18. I seldom think about my wife's per-   T   F
sonal needs.

__19. I seldom think about how to be a cre-   T   F
ative lover.

__20. I expect my wife to initiate sexual   T   F
relations.

__21. I seldom think about my wife during   T   F
the day.

__22. I seldom make an effort to know what   T   F
my wife is doing during the day—
that is, her personal work schedule.

__23. I'd rather spend most of my time by   T   F
myself.

__24. When I know I'm going to be coming   T   F
home later than normal, I usually do
not call my wife and explain what has
happened.

__25. I seldom seek my wife's consent to   T   F
do things.

(continued)

__26. I resent having to spend money on   T   F
my wife.

__27. If I had to do it over again, I'd rather   T   F
not have children.

__28. I seldom express appreciation to my   T   F
wife for her ministry to me and my
children.

__29. I resent having to work to earn a liv-   T   F
ing for for my family.

__30. I seldom postpone my desire for sex-   T   F
ual activities.

__31. I seldom spend time preparing my   T   F
wife emotionally for our sexual experience or helping her reach a sexual
climax.

__32. I seldom write love notes to my wife.   T   F

__33. Most of the time when I say, "I love   T   F
you," to my wife, it's when we're hav-
ing sexual relations.

__34. I resent the children's demands upon   T   F
my wife when I want to spend time
with her privately.

Step 2—Instructions for Both Spouses

Now that you've completed the evaluation scales designed for each of you (Scale 1), fill out the following scales (Scale 2) designed to evaluate your mate in the same areas. In other words, the following scales are designed to help each of you get your mate's perspective on the same items you just marked *true* or *false* about yourselves.

Step 2—Scale 2 For Wives About Their Husbands

Circle the "T" to indicate that you feel the statement is *mostly true* regarding your husband's behavior. Circle the "F" to indicate the statement is *mostly false* regarding your husband's behavior. *Note*: Some of the following statements may not be applicable to your situation. If so, simply mark these with an "F" (false).

___ 1. When my husband comes home   T   F
from work, he immediately seeks a place of privacy where he can do his own thing.

___ 2. When my husband comes home   T   F
from work, he wants me to be available immediately to listen to his problems.

___ 3. My husband resents it when I am   T   F
running behind schedule with my meal preparation.

___ 4. My husband does not expect to help   T   F
with the children when he's home.

___ 5. My husband seldom thinks about the   T   F
burden I carry when home all day with the children.

___ 6. When my husband wants to have   T   F
sexual relations, he seldom thinks about my personal schedule.

___ 7. My husband resents it when I get   T   F
attention.

___ 8. My husband seldom thanks me for   T   F
cooking meals and taking care of the home.

___ 9. My husband seldom suggests that   T   F
we eat out.

(over)

___10. My husband resents it when I sleep   T   F
late in the morning.

___11. My husband resents it when I stay up   T   F
late to get things done around the
house.

___12. My husband seldom asks me what   T   F
he can do to help with my work.

___13. When my husband has a day off, he   T   F
usually plans to spend it with his
male companions (golfing, playing
tennis, etc.).

___14. When my husband has a choice   T   F
between spending time with me or
his friends, he usually chooses to
spend time with his friends.

___15. When my husband has a choice   T   F
between spending time with me or
the children, he usually spends time
with the children.

___16. My husband seldom calls me during   T   F
the day and tells me he misses me
and loves me.

___17. My husband seldom thinks about   T   F
how to encourage me when he
comes home from work.

___18. My husband seldom thinks about my   T   F
personal needs.

___19. My husband seldom thinks about   T   F
how to be a creative lover.

___20. My husband expects me to initiate   T   F
sexual relations.

___21. My husband seldom thinks about me   T   F
during the day.

___22. My husband seldom makes an effort   T   F
to know what I'm doing during the
day—that is, to become aware of my
personal schedule.

(continued)

___23. My husband would rather spend   T   F
most of his time by himself.

___24. When my husband knows he's going   T   F
to be coming home later than nor-
mal, he usually does not call me and
explain what has happened.

___25. My husband seldom seeks my con-   T   F
sent to do things.

___26. My husband resents having to spend   T   F
money on me.

___27. If my husband had it to do over   T   F
again, he'd rather not have children.

___28. My husband seldom expresses   T   F
appreciation to me for my ministry to
him and the children.

___29. My husband resents having to work   T   F
to earn a living for the family.

___30. My husband seldom postpones his   T   F
desire for sexual activities.

___31. My husband seldom spends time   T   F
preparing me emotionally for our
sexual experience or helping me
reach a sexual climax.

___32. My husband seldom writes love   T   F
notes to me.

___33. Most of the time when my husband   T   F
says, "I love you," it's when we're
having sexual relations.

___34. My husband resents the children's   T   F
demands upon me when he wants to
spend time with me privately.

Step 2—Scale 2 For Husbands About Their Wives

Circle the "T" to indicate that you feel the statement is *mostly true* regarding your wife's behavior. Circle the "F" to indicate the statement is *mostly false* regarding your wife's behavior. *Note:* Some of the following statements may not be applicable to your situation. If so, simply mark these with an "F" (false).

__ 1. When I come home from work, my wife immediately asks me to sit down and listen to her problems.   T   F

__ 2. When my wife sees I have a few spare moments at home, she presents me with a list of things that she wants me to do around the house.   T   F

__ 3. My wife resents it when I sit down in the family room and watch television—especially when she's preparing a meal.   T   F

__ 4. My wife expects me to take care of the children while I'm home.   T   F

__ 5. My wife resents the fact that I am away from the children during the day and she has to take care of them.   T   F

__ 6. My wife is quite frequently emotionally resistant when I have sexual interests and needs.   T   F

__ 7. My wife resents the fact that I get more attention from others than she does.   T   F

__ 8. My wife resents having to cook meals and take care of the home.   T   F

(over)

___ 9. My wife wants to eat out most of the time.   T   F

___10. My wife sleeps late most days, getting up after I leave for work.   T   F

___11. My wife usually stays up late to do things after I go to bed.   T   F

___12. My wife seldom asks me what she can do to help me with my work.   T   F

___13. My wife spends more time with her friends than with me.   T   F

___14. When my wife has a choice between setting aside time to be with me or her friends, she usually sets aside time to be with her friends.   T   F

___15. When my wife has a choice between setting aside time to be with me or the children, she usually sets aside time to be with the children.   T   F

___16. My wife seldom calls me at work and tells me she misses me and loves me.   T   F

___17. My wife seldom plans how she can make me feel welcome when I come home.   T   F

___18. My wife seldom thinks about my personal needs.   T   F

___19. My wife seldom thinks about how to be a creative lover.   T   F

___20. My wife seldom initiates sexual relations.   T   F

___21. My wife seldom thinks about me during the day.   T   F

___22. My wife seldom makes an effort to know what I am doing during the day—that is, my personal work schedule.   T   F

(continued)

___23. My wife would rather spend most of   T   F
her time by herself.

___24. When my wife knows she's going to   T   F
be gone when I come home, she
usually does not leave a note of
explanation or call me and explain
changes in her personal scheduling.

___25. My wife seldom seeks my consent to   T   F
do things.

___26. My wife resents the fact that she   T   F
doesn't have a separate bank
account.

___27. If my wife had to do it over again, she   T   F
would rather not have children.

___28. My wife seldom thanks me for my   T   F
commitment to my job and providing
materially for her personal needs.

___29. My wife resents having to care for   T   F
children, keep up the home, prepare
meals, etc.

___30. My wife resents my sexual requests.   T   F

___31. My wife resents the fact that I am ful-   T   F
filled sexually.

___32. My wife seldom writes love notes to   T   F
me.

___33. My wife seldom tells me how much   T   F
she loves me.

___34. My wife resents the children's   T   F
demands upon me when she wants
to spend time with me privately.

Step 3—Instructions for Both Spouses

Now that both of you have completed the two previous scales, compare your evaluation of your mate (Scale 2) with your mate's self-evaluation (Scale 1). To identify areas of discrepancy as well as areas of agreement, record your mate's answers on the following scales.

Step 3—Scale 3: Wife's Scale Compared with Husband's Evaluation

This form is to be used once you have completed both the evaluation scale designed for you as a wife (Scale 1 for Wives) and the one your husband filled out on you (Scale 2 for Husbands). Record both sets of answers in the blanks provided in the two columns following each item. This will enable you to see how your evaluation of yourself compares with your mate's evaluation of you.

	Exercise 1 for Wives	Exercise 2 for Husbands
__ 1. When my husband comes home from work, I immediately ask him to sit down and listen to my problems.	____	____
__ 2. When I see my husband has a few spare moments at home, I present him with a list of things that I want him to do around the house.	____	____
__ 3. I resent it when my husband sits down in the family room and watches television—especially when I'm preparing a meal.	____	____
__ 4. I expect my husband to take care of the children while he's home.	____	____
__ 5. I resent the fact that my husband is away from the children during the day and I have to take care of them.	____	____
__ 6. I find myself quite frequently emotionally resistant when I know my husband has sexual interests and needs.	____	____

(over)

__ 7. I resent the fact that my husband gets more attention from others than I do.   ___   ___

__ 8. I resent having to cook meals and take care of the home.   ___   ___

__ 9. I want to eat out most of the time.   ___   ___

__10. I sleep late most days, getting up after my husband leaves for work.   ___   ___

__11. I usually stay up late to do things after my husband goes to bed.   ___   ___

__12. I seldom ask my husband what I can do to help him with his work.   ___   ___

__13. I spend more time with my friends than with my husband.   ___   ___

__14. When I have a choice between setting aside time to be with my husband or my friends, I usually set aside time to be with my friends.   ___   ___

__15. When I have a choice between setting aside time to be with my husband or my children, I usually set aside time to be with my children.   ___   ___

__16. I seldom call my husband at work and tell him I miss him and love him.   ___   ___

__17. I seldom plan how I can make my husband feel welcome when he comes home.   ___   ___

__18. I seldom think about my husband's personal needs.   ___   ___

(continued)

___19. I seldom think about how to be a creative lover.

___20. I seldom initiate sexual relations.

___21. I seldom think about my husband during the day.

___22. I seldom make an effort to know what my husband is doing during the day—that is, his personal work schedule.

___23. I'd rather spend most of my time by myself.

___24. When I know I'm going to be gone when my husband comes home, I usually do not leave a note of explanation or call him and explain changes in my personal scheduling.

___25. I seldom seek my husband's consent to do things.

___26. I resent the fact that I don't have a separate bank account.

___27. If I had to do it over again, I'd rather not have children.

___28. I seldom thank my husband for his commitment to his job and providing materially for my personal needs.

___29. I resent having to care for children, keep up the home, prepare meals, etc.

___30. I resent my husband's sexual requests.

___31. I resent the fact that my husband is fulfilled sexually.

(over)

__32. I seldom write love notes to   ____   ____
     my husband.
__33. I seldom tell my husband   ____   ____
     how much I love him.
__34. I   resent   the   children's   ____   ____
     demands upon my husband
     when I want to spend time
     with him privately.

Step 3—Scale 3: Husband's Scale Compared with Wife's Evaluation

This form is to be used once you have completed both the evaluation scale designed for you as a husband (Scale 1 for Husbands) and the one your wife filled out on you (Scale 2 for Wives). Record both sets of answers in the blanks provided in the two columns following each item. This will enable you to see how your evaluation of yourself compares with your mate's evaluation of you.

	Exercise 1 for Husbands	Exercise 2 for Wives
__ 1. When I come home from work, I immediately seek a place of privacy where I can do my own thing.	____	____
__ 2. When I come home from work, I want my wife to be available immediately to listen to my problems.	____	____
__ 3. I resent it when my wife is running behind in meal preparation.	____	____
__ 4. I do not expect to help with the children when I'm home.	____	____
__ 5. I seldom think about the burden my wife carries when she is home all day with the children.	____	____
__ 6. When I want to have sexual relations with my wife, I seldom think about her personal schedule.	____	____
__ 7. I resent it when my wife gets attention.	____	____

(over)

__ 8. I seldom thank my wife for cooking meals and taking care of the home.   ____   ____

__ 9. I seldom suggest to my wife that we eat out.   ____   ____

__10. I resent it when my wife sleeps late in the morning.   ____   ____

__11. I resent it when my wife stays up late to get things done around the house.   ____   ____

__12. I seldom ask my wife what I can do to help her with her work.   ____   ____

__13. When I have a day off, I usually plan to spend it with my male companions (golfing, playing tennis, etc.).   ____   ____

__14. When I have a choice between spending time with my wife or my friends, I usually choose to spend time with my friends.   ____   ____

__15. When I have a choice between spending time with my wife or my children, I usually choose to spend time with my children.   ____   ____

__16. I seldom call my wife during the day and tell her I miss her and love her.   ____   ____

__17. I seldom think about how I can encourage my wife when I come home from work.   ____   ____

__18. I seldom think about my wife's personal needs.   ____   ____

__19. I seldom think about how to be a creative lover.   ____   ____

(continued)

—20. I expect my wife to initiate sexual relations.

—21. I seldom think about my wife during the day.

—22. I seldom make an effort to know what my wife is doing during the day—that is, her personal work schedule.

—23. I'd rather spend most of my time by myself.

—24. When I know I'm going to be coming home later than normal, I usually do not call my wife and explain what has happened.

—25. I seldom seek my wife's consent to do things.

—26. I resent having to spend money on my wife.

—27. If I had to do it over again, I'd rather not have children.

—28. I seldom express appreciation to my wife for her ministry to me and my children.

—29. I resent having to work to earn a living for for my family.

—30. I seldom postpone my desire for sexual activities.

—31. I seldom spend time preparing my wife emotionally for our sexual experience or helping her reach a sexual climax.

—32. I seldom write love notes to my wife.

(continued)

_33. Most of the time when I say, "I   ____   ____
love you," to my wife, it's
when we're having sexual
relations.

_34. I resent the children's   ____   ____
demands upon my wife when
I want to spend time with her
privately.

Step 4—Instructions for Both Spouses

Now that you both have recorded your answers on the forms designed for comparative study (Scale 3), isolate the areas of discrepancy by placing a check (✔) in the space provided before each statement on Scale 3.

Then discuss the areas of discrepancy and why you think they exist. Do so as sensitively and nondefensively as possible.

Step 5—Instructions for Both Spouses

Following your discussion of the comparative study (Step 4), each of you should go through the original evaluation scale (Scale 1), designed for each of you and place a check (✔) in the space provided beside each item that you marked "T" for *mostly true* about yourself.

Note: Answers you've marked "T" about yourself indicate areas of life that usually (but not always) focus on yourself rather than the other partner. Utilizing your observations from both the comparative studies as well as your personal scales, you are now ready to set up personal goals for your marriage.

Step 6—Instructions for Both Spouses

Utilizing the observations you've both made in your comparative study as well as on your personal evaluation scales, write out specific goals for yourselves as marital partners. Use the following worksheets for setting these goals.

Caution

Each marital partner is entitled to his own rights in a marriage. To say we have no rights is an oversimplification. For example, a wife needs a husband who will sit down and listen to her problems; also, a husband needs the same attention. However, if we consistently demand this right, we have put the primary focus on ourselves rather than on our mate. To do so violates Jesus' example, who came to minister rather than to be ministered unto. God's will is that both mates reach out to the other to meet each other's needs. When we do so, our own needs will be met. The relationship is then in proper focus.

Step 6—Wife's Worksheet for Setting Goals

Instructions: Set your goals based on changes you would like to make in order to love your husband more like Christ has loved you. For example, if you consistently ask your husband to sit down and listen to your problems the moment he gets home from work (item 1), your goals might read: "I will do all I can to make it possible for my husband to have some private time to relax and unwind when he comes home from work before I share with him my own personal needs and problems."

Or, if you purposely stay up late (item 11) to avoid meeting your husband's sexual needs (item 30), your goal might read: "I will, as much as possible, plan to get necessary tasks completed so that I can retire when my husband does."

Note: It is understood, of course, that all of us can improve in most all of the areas mentioned on the evaluation scales. However, the checked items (✔), both on your "personal evaluation scale" and on the "comparative study form," will reveal areas that need improvement. Concentrate on the significant areas in your goal setting.

1. I will . . .

2. I will . . .

(over)

3. I will . . .

4. I will . . .

5. I will . . .

Step 6—Husband's Worksheet for Setting Goals

Instructions: Set your goals based on changes you would like to make in order to love your wife more like Christ has loved you. For example, if you always seek a place of privacy when you come home from work so you don't have to listen to your wife share her own personal needs and problems (item 1), your goal might read: "I will plan to be available to my wife when I come home from work to give her a few minutes to share her own personal needs and problems."

Or, if you seldom spend time preparing your wife emotionally for her sexual experience (item 31), your goal might read: "I will do all I can to understand my wife's emotional needs and how this relates to her feelings about sex. I will then do all I can to meet those needs."

Note: It is understood, of course, that all of us can improve in most all of the areas mentioned on the evaluation scales. However, the checked items (✔), both on your "personal evaluation scale" and on the "comparative study form," will reveal areas that need improvement. Concentrate on the significant areas in your goal setting.

1. I will . . .

2. I will . . .

(over)

3. I will . . .

4. I will . . .

5. I will . . .

Step 7—Instructions for Both Spouses

Conclude in prayer. You may wish to use Paul's prayer for the Ephesians, applying what he says to the experience that you've just had:

> *For this reason I kneel before the Father, from whom his whole family in heaven and on earth derives its name. I pray that out of his glorious riches he may strengthen you with power through his Spirit in your inner being, so that Christ may dwell in your hearts through faith. And I pray that you, being rooted and established in love, may have power, together with all the saints, to grasp how wide and long and high and deep is the love of Christ, and to know this love that surpasses knowledge— that you may be filled to the measure of all the fullness of God* (Eph. 3:14-19, *NIV*).

Note
1. For a careful exegetical analysis of the Hebrew text in Genesis 3:14-16, see Ronald C. Allen's *Majesty of Man* (Portland, OR: Multnomah Press, 1984), p. 147.

4

SUBMITTING TO EACH OTHER

No aspect of marriage has been given more universal attention than wifely submission. And, of course, it is a very controversial subject at this juncture in our present-day cultural journey—particularly among those who classify themselves as feminists or who, at least, are sympathetic to feminist ideology.

The very word *submission* is threatening. One reason is that we haven't understood its meaning as we should. We sometimes think of submission as allowing another person to dominate and control us. All of us resist that kind of relationship.

In God's scheme of things, the concept of submission was never to be applicable to only one person in a given relationship. It was to be reciprocal and mutual.

It must be added that there are times when a marital partner (or any person) may need to submit under conditions that are not reciprocal. But God never intended this to be the normal rule for any human being, particularly since Christ came and introduced a whole new way of life.

What the Bible Says

The fact is that the Bible does teach submission, but not only for wives. It is a quality of life that should character-ize all of us in our relationships with others. Thus, Paul, before exhorting wives to be submissive to their hus-bands (see Eph. 5:22), exhorted *all* believers to be "sub-ject [to submit] to one another in the fear of Christ" (Eph. 5:21).

It's interesting that Paul did not use the word *submis-sion* in his statement to wives. Rather, he based his directive for wives to submit on his use of the word in verse 21 when he was speaking to all the followers of Christ in Ephesus. In other words, Paul told all of these people they were to submit to one another, including wives to husbands (5:22), husbands to wives (5:25), chil-dren to parents (6:1), fathers to children (6:4), servants to masters (6:5) and masters to servants (6:9). Put another way, Paul's statement to submit to one another in verse 21 is the basic concept on which he builds his specific exhortations to the other people mentioned in the remaining part of his Ephesian letter.

Christ demonstrated His love by becoming a servant, and it is impossible to be a servant without being submissive.

That Paul believed husbands should submit to their wives is clearly illustrated in the fact that they are directed to love as Christ loved. As we've already seen from Philippians, Christ demonstrated His love by becoming a servant, and it is impossible to be a servant without being submissive. Inherent, then, in Paul's state-ment to love as Christ loved is a submissive attitude and spirit.

Don't misunderstand. Discussion and dialogue and

even disagreement are not necessarily synonymous with a nonsubmissive attitude. It depends on how it is done. Those who classify all resistance as nonsubmissive do not understand the communication process. God forbid that a man never allow his wife to disagree with him. If he does, he, at that moment, also becomes nonsubmissive and certainly is not loving as Christ loved. Unfortunately, some husbands have interpreted Paul's injunction to wives in this narrow way, which is incorrect and quite fre-

---

If a husband and wife continually love each other as Christ loved them and regularly fulfill their God-ordained responsibilities and trust each other, they have the potential to experience a growing unity and oneness that can actually be a foretaste of heaven on this side of glory.

---

quently rooted in personal pride and insecurity. In short, it reflects a male ego that has not been brought into conformity with Christ's example of love and way of life.

A Larger Perspective

Some theological background will help clarify further why Paul emphasized submission for women in general and wives in particular. First, God created Eve for Adam. She was not to be his subordinate, but his equal. However, when sin entered the world, Eve (and all women following her) had to bear a special burden because Eve was first deceived (see 1 Tim. 2:13,14). If we are to accept the biblical account at all, we cannot deny these facts. This view is not just merely a Pauline interpretation but, rather, this concept can be traced all the way through the Bible. Furthermore, history verifies this reality.

However, with the coming of Jesus Christ, something unique happened regarding a woman's role. As Christians, a man and wife have the potential to experience a unity and oneness that can grow constantly deeper and more meaningful day by day. From God's eternal and spiritual perspective, there's total equality (see Gal. 3:28). But, since marriage is not an eternal relationship and is limited to time and space, man was appointed to be the head (as Christ is the head of the Church) and the woman is to recognize his God-given authority. Becoming Christians does not mean we never sin. But, in Christ, if a husband and wife continually love each other as Christ loved them and regularly fulfill their God-ordained responsibilities and trust each other, they have the potential to experience a growing unity and oneness that can actually be a foretaste of heaven on this side of glory.

Throughout history there have been reactions and overreactions to God's plan. Much of it has been based on misinterpretation of Scripture, which, in itself, reflects the influence of sin on our lives. Unfortunately, we even tend to interpret Scripture in order to benefit ourselves.

The only answer to these misinterpretations and over-reactions is to follow Christ's example and instructions. Then husbands can love their wives as Christ loved the Church, which includes submission. And wives can submit to their husbands as the Church is subject to Christ, which certainly includes loving as Christ loved. In fact, Christ's love is the basis for mutual submission. And mutual submission is possible without eliminating the husband's headship. Applying these biblical principles is the only way to experience functional egalitarianism and equality and still maintain the husband/wife roles specified in Scripture.

An Exercise in Submitting

Marriage, more than any other relationship, includes many areas calling for mutual submission.
• What are these areas?
• To what extent are you submissive?
• Why are you having difficulty submitting?
• In what ways do you make it difficult for your mate to submit to you?
• How can you become a more submissive person?
This section is designed to help you answer these questions.

Step 1—Instructions for Both Spouses

As a husband and wife, complete the following "Submission Scale for Wives" and "Submission Scale for Husbands."

Step 1—Scale 1: A Submission Scale for Wives

Instructions: Circle the number that best describes your attitudes and actions toward your husband. If the statement describes an attitude and action that is seldom a problem, you should circle a low number. If it describes an attitude and action that tends to be a problem, you should circle a high number.

I find it difficult to submit when . . .

	Never a Problem						Always a Problem
1. My husband asks me to do things that are routine and boring.	1	2	3	4	5	6	7
2. My husband asks me to be more frugal in spending money.	1	2	3	4	5	6	7
3. My husband asks me to be neater in personal grooming.	1	2	3	4	5	6	7
4. My husband asks me directly or indirectly to meet his sexual needs.	1	2	3	4	5	6	7
5. My husband asks me to break a personal habit.	1	2	3	4	5	6	7
6. My husband asks me to be more orderly regarding my personal life.	1	2	3	4	5	6	7
7. My husband asks me to give up something I plan to do in order to do something he wants to do.	1	2	3	4	5	6	7
8. My husband asks me to set goals for my life and the family.	1	2	3	4	5	6	7
9. My husband asks for a period of time to communicate.	1	2	3	4	5	6	7
10. My husband asks me to do something immediately when I'm planning to do it later.	1	2	3	4	5	6	7

(over)

11. My husband asks me to do something I usually do anyway.   1 2 3 4 5 6 7

12. My husband asks me directly or indirectly to be more creative in our lovemaking.   1 2 3 4 5 6 7

13. My husband asks me to do something I feel is his responsibility.   1 2 3 4 5 6 7

14. My husband asks me to help with the children.   1 2 3 4 5 6 7

15. My husband asks me to help with his work.   1 2 3 4 5 6 7

16. My husband asks me to explain my personal schedule.   1 2 3 4 5 6 7

17. Other _____   1 2 3 4 5 6 7

18. Other _____   1 2 3 4 5 6 7

19. Other _____   1 2 3 4 5 6 7

20. Other _____   1 2 3 4 5 6 7

Step 1—Scale 1: A Submission Scale for Husbands

Instructions: Circle the number that best describes your attitudes and actions toward your wife. If the statement describes an attitude and action that is seldom a problem, you should circle a low number. If it describes an attitude and action that tends to be a problem, you should circle a high number.

I find it difficult to submit when . . .

	Never a Problem						Always a Problem
1. My wife asks me to do things that are routine and boring.	1	2	3	4	5	6	7
2. My wife asks me to be more frugal in spending money.	1	2	3	4	5	6	7
3. My wife asks me to be neater in personal grooming.	1	2	3	4	5	6	7
4. My wife asks me directly or indirectly to meet her sexual needs.	1	2	3	4	5	6	7
5. My wife asks me to break a personal habit.	1	2	3	4	5	6	7
6. My wife asks me to be more orderly regarding my personal life.	1	2	3	4	5	6	7
7. My wife asks me to give up something I plan to do in order to do something she wants to do.	1	2	3	4	5	6	7
8. My wife asks me to set goals for my life and the family.	1	2	3	4	5	6	7
9. My wife asks for a period of time to communicate.	1	2	3	4	5	6	7
10. My wife asks me to do something immediately when I'm planning to do it later.	1	2	3	4	5	6	7

(over)

11. My wife asks me to do something I usually do anyway.   1 2 3 4 5 6 7

12. My wife asks me directly or indirectly to be more creative in our lovemaking.   1 2 3 4 5 6 7

13. My wife asks me to do something I feel is her responsibility.   1 2 3 4 5 6 7

14. My wife asks me to help with the children.   1 2 3 4 5 6 7

15. My wife asks me to help with her work.   1 2 3 4 5 6 7

16. My wife asks me to explain my personal schedule.   1 2 3 4 5 6 7

17. Other _____

18. Other _____   1 2 3 4 5 6 7

19. Other _____   1 2 3 4 5 6 7

20. Other _____   1 2 3 4 5 6 7

Step 2—Instructions for Both Spouses

Now that you've completed the "Submission Scale for Wives" and the "Submission Scale for Husbands," use the following scales to evaluate each other.

Wives, complete "Scale 2: A Submission Scale for Wives: About Their Husbands". Husbands, complete "Scale 2: A Submission Scale for Husbands: About Their Wives".

Step 2—Scale 2: For Wives: About Their Husbands

My husband finds it difficult to submit when . . .

	Never a Problem					Always a Problem

1. I ask him to do things that are routine and boring. 1 2 3 4 5 6 7
2. I ask him to be more frugal in spending money. 1 2 3 4 5 6 7
3. I ask him to be neater in personal grooming. 1 2 3 4 5 6 7
4. I ask him directly or indirectly to meet my sexual needs. 1 2 3 4 5 6 7
5. I ask him to break a personal habit. 1 2 3 4 5 6 7
6. I ask him to be more orderly regarding his personal life. 1 2 3 4 5 6 7
7. I ask him to give up something he plans to do in order to do something I want to do. 1 2 3 4 5 6 7
8. I ask him to set goals for his life and the family. 1 2 3 4 5 6 7
9. I ask for a period of time to communicate. 1 2 3 4 5 6 7
10. I ask him to do something immediately when he's planning to do it later. 1 2 3 4 5 6 7
11. I ask him to do something he usually does anyway. 1 2 3 4 5 6 7
12. I ask him directly or indirectly to be more creative in our lovemaking. 1 2 3 4 5 6 7
13. I ask him to do something he feels is my responsibility. 1 2 3 4 5 6 7
14. I ask him to help with the children. 1 2 3 4 5 6 7
15. I ask him to help me with my work. 1 2 3 4 5 6 7
16. I ask him to explain his personal schedule. 1 2 3 4 5 6 7
17. Other _____ 1 2 3 4 5 6 7
18. Other _____ 1 2 3 4 5 6 7
19. Other _____ 1 2 3 4 5 6 7
20. Other _____ 1 2 3 4 5 6 7

Step 2—Scale 2: For Husbands: About Their Wives

My wife finds it difficult to submit when . . .

	Never a Problem						Always a Problem
1. I ask her to do things that are routine and boring.	1	2	3	4	5	6	7
2. I ask her to be more frugal in spending money.	1	2	3	4	5	6	7
3. I ask her to be neater in personal grooming.	1	2	3	4	5	6	7
4. I ask her directly or indirectly to meet my sexual needs.	1	2	3	4	5	6	7
5. I ask her to break a personal habit.	1	2	3	4	5	6	7
6. I ask her to be more orderly regarding her personal life.	1	2	3	4	5	6	7
7. I ask her to give up something she plans to do in order to do something I want to do.	1	2	3	4	5	6	7
8. I ask her to set goals for her life and the family.	1	2	3	4	5	6	7
9. I ask for a period of time to communicate.	1	2	3	4	5	6	7
10. I ask her to do something immediately when she's planning to do it later.	1	2	3	4	5	6	7
11. I ask her to do something she usually does anyway.	1	2	3	4	5	6	7
12. I ask her directly or indirectly to be more creative in our lovemaking.	1	2	3	4	5	6	7
13. I ask her to do something she feels is my responsibility.	1	2	3	4	5	6	7
14. I ask her to help with the children.	1	2	3	4	5	6	7
15. I ask her to help me with my work.	1	2	3	4	5	6	7
16. I ask her to explain her personal schedule.	1	2	3	4	5	6	7
17. Other _____	1	2	3	4	5	6	7
18. Other _____	1	2	3	4	5	6	7
19. Other _____	1	2	3	4	5	6	7
20. Other _____	1	2	3	4	5	6	7

Step 3—Instructions for Both Spouses

Now that you've evaluated yourself personally as well as each other, compare your answers. To do this, fill in the blanks beside each item on the following comparative forms (Scale 3).

Step 3—Scale 3 For Wives: A Personal Evaluation of Herself Compared with Her Husband's Evaluation of Her

This form is to be used once you have completed the evaluation scale designed for you as a wife, "Scale 1 for Wives," and the one your husband filled out on you, "Scale 2 for Husbands." Record the numbers in the blanks provided in the two columns.

	Scale 1 My Personal Evaluation of Myself	Scale 2 My Husband's Evaluation of Me

I find it difficult to submit when . . .

___ 1. My mate asks me to do things that are routine and boring.

___ 2. My mate asks me to be more frugal in spending money.

___ 3. My mate asks me to be neater in personal grooming.

___ 4. My mate asks me directly or indirectly to meet his sexual needs.

___ 5. My mate asks me to break a personal habit.

___ 6. My mate asks me to be more orderly regarding my personal life.

___ 7. My mate asks me to give up something I plan to do in order to do something he wants to do.

(over)

__ 8. My mate asks me to set _____   _____
goals for my life and
the family.

__ 9. My mate asks for a per- _____   _____
iod of time to communi-
cate.

__10. My mate asks me to do _____   _____
something immediately
when I'm planning to
do it later.

__11. My mate asks me to do _____   _____
something I usually do
anyway.

__12. My mate asks me   _____   _____
directly or indirectly to
be more creative in our
lovemaking.

__13. My mate asks me to do _____   _____
something I feel is his
responsibility.

__14. My mate asks me to   _____   _____
help with the children.

__15. My mate asks me to   _____   _____
help with his work.

__16. My mate asks me to   _____   _____
explain my personal
schedule.

__17. Other _____   _____   _____
__18. Other _____   _____   _____
__19. Other _____   _____   _____
__20. Other _____   _____   _____

Step 3—Scale 3: For Husbands: A Personal Evaluation of Himself Compared with His Wife's Evaluation of Him

This form is to be used once you have completed the evaluation scale designed for you as a husband, "Scale 1 for Husbands," and the one your wife filled out on you, "Scale 2 for Wives." Record the numbers in the blanks provided in the two columns.

	Scale 1 My Personal Evaluation of Myself	Scale 2 My Wife's Evaluation of Me

I find it difficult to submit when . . .

— 1. My mate asks me to do things that are are routine and boring.

— 2. My mate asks me to be more frugal in spending money.

— 3. My mate asks me to be neater in personal grooming.

— 4. My mate asks me directly or indirectly to meet her sexual needs.

— 5. My mate asks me to break a personal habit.

— 6. My mate asks me to be more orderly regarding my personal life.

— 7. My mate asks me to give up something I plan to do in order to do something she wants to do.

(over)

— 8. My mate asks me to set _____   _____
     goals for my life and
     the family.

— 9. My mate asks for a per- _____   _____
     iod of time to communi-
     cate.

—10. My mate asks me to do _____   _____
     something immediately
     when I'm planning to
     do it later.

—11. My mate asks me to do _____   _____
     something I usually do
     anyway.

—12. My mate asks me   _____   _____
     directly or indirectly to
     be more creative in our
     lovemaking.

—13. My mate asks me to do _____   _____
     something I feel is her
     responsibility.

—14. My mate asks me to   _____   _____
     help with the children.

—15. My mate asks me to   _____   _____
     help with her work.

—16. My mate asks me to   _____   _____
     explain my personal
     schedule.

—17. Other _____   _____   _____
—18. Other _____   _____   _____
—19. Other _____   _____   _____
—20. Other _____   _____   _____

Step 4—Instructions for Both Spouses

Compare your answers by placing a check (✔) in the space provided by each item in Scale 3 where there are two or more points of difference in your evaluations. Then sensitively discuss with each other why you believe this variance exists. Take turns sharing and listening to each other. Then discuss together as objectively as possible how you can help each other more easily submit to each other's desires.

Note: If you cannot work through this project satisfactorily, arriving at a degree of mutual understanding and concern for each other, you no doubt need to seek help from your pastor or a professional marriage counselor. The sooner you do so, the better.

Step 5—Instructions for Both Spouses

On the basis of your observations and discussions together, write out personal goals in two areas—ways in which you will be more submissive and ways in which you will help your mate to be more submissive.

Step 5—Personal Goals for Wives

As you state your goals, answer two questions:
- In what areas can I be more submissive to my husband?
- In what ways can I help my husband be more submissive to me?

1. I will be more submissive to my husband by:

   a.

   b.

   c.

2. I will help my husband be more submissive to me by:

   a.

   b.

   c.

Step 5—Personal Goals for Husbands

As you state your goals, answer two questions:
- In what areas can I be more submissive to my wife?
- In what ways can I help my wife be more submissive to me?

1. I will be more submissive to my wife by:

   a.

   b.

   c.

2. I will help my wife be more submissive to me by:

   a.

   b.

   c.

Step 6—Instructions for Both Spouses

As a couple, use Paul's prayer for the Romans, applying it to your own relationship!

> "Now may the God who gives perseverance and encouragement grant us to be of the same mind with one another according to Christ Jesus, that with one accord we may with one voice glorify the God and Father of our Lord Jesus Christ" (Rom. 15:5,6 paraphrase).

5
LEARNING TO LOVE

A couple was having serious problems in their marriage. One of the pastors in our church met with the husband one day for lunch and very pointedly asked him if he loved his wife.

"Yes," he responded, "I love her."

"May I read something to you?" asked the pastor. He opened his Bible and read from 1 Corinthians 13, which outlines the qualities Paul defined as love:

- Love is patient
- Love is kind
- Love does not envy
- Love does not boast
- Love is not proud
- Love is not rude
- Love is not self-seeking
- Love is not easily angered
- Love keeps no record of wrongs
- Love does not delight in evil
- Love rejoices in the truth

- Love always protects
- Love always trusts
- Love always hopes
- Love always perseveres.

After the pastor had read this list from 1 Corinthians 13:4-8, he asked the question again, "Do you really love your wife?"

Without a moment's hesitation the husband responded, "No, I really don't love my wife—not that way!"

You see, the man's first response was based on our contemporary culture's definition of love—primarily, sexual feelings. And, in this case, which can be multiplied again and again, what this man defined as *love* was probably not love at all.

Unfortunately, our Western culture particularly has propagated the idea that feelings of attraction, especially sexual feelings, are the essence of love. This is a very superficial and inadequate explanation of what keeps a marital relationship on track. In many instances, what is initially classified as love is a selfish feeling—a desire to have the other person satisfy a personal need.

Agapao Love

The words *agapao* and *agape* are used most frequently in the New Testament to describe love. In most instances, these Greek words are used to portray loving acts—that is, behaving in certain ways because it is the right thing to do. Though agape love should normally be combined with positive feelings, it is the kind of love that should cause us to meet our mate's needs, no matter how we personally feel.

Experience bears out why this kind of love must form the foundation for every marriage. If we performed our responsibilities to each other only when we felt like it, we would frequently leave undone many important things that contribute to marital harmony. For example, a man who faces a really tough day in the office in order to earn money to provide for his family does not always—at least at that moment—attack his responsibilities with strong motivation and positive emotions. But, if he really behaves toward his wife and family as Christ loved him, he'll do what is right, in spite of his negative feelings.

Men and women who indeed love according to God's perspective and Christ's example are able to work through situations with sensitivity, maturity and good balance.

The same is true of wives and mothers. Washing clothes, preparing meals and cleaning the house are not always the most exciting responsibilities. And it is even less exciting for a husband to lend a helping hand when he has just faced a day at the office that has been difficult and draining. When a husband asks his wife—who has had a difficult day at home—for help with some of his office work, her own emotions don't usually cry out with anticipation to cooperate.

Husbands and wives who are mature intellectually know there are difficult moments in marriage. And because they are mature psychologically and spiritually, their love for each other ultimately transcends their selfish tendencies. They often perform responsibilities for each other in spite of their negative feelings. In fact, meeting each other's needs in times like these is the fastest way to feel good about ourselves and our marital roles.

On the other hand, agape love also causes husbands and wives to be sensitive to each other's emotional moods. There are times when the most loving thing to do is not to place demands on our mate. At the same time, the most loving thing to do in response may mean not taking advantage of our mate's willingness to forego a need, be it emotional, social, spiritual or physical. In fact, our mate's willingness to forego a need may actually cause us to want to meet that need—if not then, as soon as it is more convenient. Acts of unselfishness in marriage actually generate positive responses. We must be careful, however, never to use this method to be manipulative.

Men and women who indeed love according to God's perspective and Christ's example are able to work through these situations with sensitivity, maturity and good balance. They're very much aware that marital life is not always a rose garden.

Phileo Love

The Greek word *phileo* is often used interchangeably in the New Testament with *agapao*, but is also used distinctively to refer to love that is emotionally positive in nature. It is associated with true friendship. It involves delight and pleasure in doing something. Perhaps one of the best definitions of this kind of love is "a deep emotional feeling of trust generated from one person to another person."[1]

This is the kind of love Paul is referring to in Romans 12:10 when he writes: "Be devoted to one another in *brotherly love.*" The Greek word translated "brotherly love" is *philadelphia*. It involves the idea of phileo love toward family members. But, in this context, Paul was using the kind of loving relationships that should exist among family members to illustrate the kind of relationships that should also exist among members of God's family.

In Christ, husbands and wives are also brothers and

sisters. They, too, are to be devoted to one another in brotherly love. And this is a special kind of love. Paul made this clear when he used the phrase "be devoted," which literally refers to the mutual affection that should exist between husbands and wives as well as other family members. Consequently, the *King James Version* reads, "Be kindly *affectioned* one to another with brotherly love," and *Beck* translates, "Love one another *tenderly* as fellow Christians."

This leads to a very important observation. The Bible uses different words to describe love. Though they are not always mutually exclusive in meaning, there are some important distinctions that relate to the subject before us—learning to love.

This distinction seems to be most clearly seen in Paul's instructions to women in Titus 2:3,4. "Likewise," Paul wrote, "teach the older women" and "then they can train the younger women *to love their husbands*" (*NIV*). This phrase is translated from the basic Greek word *philandros*.

Note that Paul assumes in these instructions to women in his letter to Titus that phileo love can be learned. In other words, we can engage not only in proper behavior toward our mate, but also develop positive feelings, particularly when we have positive models in other people.

Erao Love

There's another word for love that was used by Greek-speaking people in the first century—the word *erao*. Usually, it referred to sexual love. Interestingly, this word is never used by New Testament authors. This does not mean that sexual love is wrong or improper, or is never referred to in the New Testament. However, biblical writers, no doubt, avoided this word because it was so frequently used in their culture to describe illicit sexual activity. Though it is not totally an accurate comparison, there are certain words for sexual expressions in our present-day culture that we avoid in most proper public discussions of sexual love. Though these words are frequently used by people to describe and talk about illicit sex in literature, movies and jokes, they're considered unacceptable because of this illicit association.

Erotic experience, nevertheless, is an important part of marital love. Without it, marriage can never be what God intended it to be. It's that dimension of our personalities that enables a man and woman to be emotionally attracted to each other in ways that go beyond feelings of friendship. It enables a husband and wife to enjoy each other at levels of communication that are biblically off limits among men and women generally and family members particularly.

This does not mean that erotic feelings will not emerge under certain conditions that can lead to improper sexual behavior. The same human capacities that are designed by God to be used properly often lead to premarital sexual activity, extramarital affairs, homosexual relationships and even incest. The important point is that when a man or woman engages in erotic lovemaking, they do so according to God's will. They should avoid conditions that lead to illicit sexual behavior. And if, on occasion, sexual feelings emerge (which, in themselves, are not wrong), they should avoid the inappropriate mental and physical actions that can easily follow.

As stated earlier, our present culture often defines love in emotional and sexual terms. For example, the words of most popular songs that speak of male and female relationships are clearly focused on sexual feelings. The theme of most movies, books and magazines that feature relationships between men and women also focus on this kind of love. Consequently, when a man says to a woman, "I love you," and the woman says, "I love you, too," the essence of their feelings at that moment are frequently sexual. And, more recently in our own culture, this kind of definition of love is openly featured in homosexual relationships.

A Total Perspective

The Scriptures present the concept of love as three-dimensional. In its broadest meaning, it involves attitudes and actions that are right and proper, no matter how we feel (see fig. 1 in this chapter). Agapao love rises above feelings that may be more negative than positive. As previously stated, this is the kind of love Jesus Christ demonstrated when He, with an act of His will, chose the cross. In His humanity, He agonized over this decision. He actually prayed that He might be released from the suffering that lay ahead (see Luke 22:42). However, He knew what His Father's will was and He died on the cross, though every ounce of human emotion within His being cried out for deliverance. He willingly gave up His life for others.

It is God's will for all Christians in all relationships to "live a life of love, just as Christ loved us and gave himself up for us as a fragrant offering and sacrifice to God" (Eph. 5:2, NIV).

This is the ultimate in agape love. And it is God's will for all Christians in all relationships to "live a life of love, just as Christ loved us and gave himself up for us as a fragrant offering and sacrifice to God" (Eph. 5:2, *NIV*). This particularly applies to marriage partners.

Phileo love involves positive feelings and should always be a part of and guided by agape love (see fig. 1). In fact, it is agape love that keeps feelings of affection

from becoming selfish and demanding. Many friendships have been destroyed by people who try to keep a
relationship entirely to themselves.

This also happens in marriage. Both husbands and
wives need friendships with other men and women. A
jealous spouse can literally destroy and crush a relationship, turning it into a nightmare of emotional pain. On the
other hand, marital partners who indeed love according
to God's standards will never allow friendships outside
the marriage to interfere with their marriage. Mature
Christians who are guided by agape love, as it is defined
in the Bible, will maintain this intricate balance.

Erotic feelings and actions are also a part of the circle
of biblical love. Erao love has been designed by God to
be used and enjoyed fully, but it is always to be
expressed within the boundaries of agapao and phileo
love (see fig. 1). It is this larger context that keeps a relationship morally on track. And it is only this larger context
that will keep these feelings from being used in selfish
ways, even in a marital relationship. Furthermore, it is this
larger context that helps a married couple keep their
emotional equilibrium during the many times when married life is difficult and demanding.

THE CIRCLE OF BIBLICAL LOVE

Doing what is right and best for someone, even if it involves negative feelings.

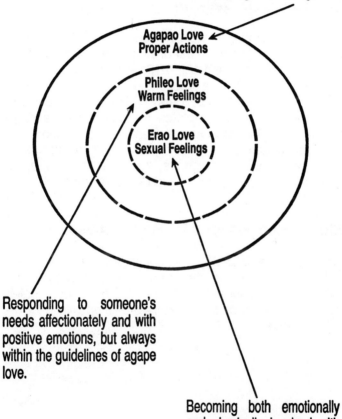

Agapao Love
Proper Actions

Phileo Love
Warm Feelings

Erao Love
Sexual Feelings

Responding to someone's needs affectionately and with positive emotions, but always within the guidelines of agape love.

Becoming both emotionally and physically involved with another person sexually, but always within the guidelines of agape and phileo love.

An Exercise in Developing Action Love

There is no simple formula for learning to love another person in a total sense. First of all, it requires being obedient to God (see John 15:10-12) and, many times, that is a difficult assignment emotionally.

First Corinthians 13 probably outlines the dimensions of agape love more completely than any other passage of Scripture. The following evaluation assignments are designed to help you measure your growth in expressing agape love toward your mate, and then to set specific goals in areas where you would like to improve.

Step 1—Instructions for Both Spouses

Complete the following evaluation scales, which are designed to indicate the degree of agape love you exhibit toward your mate. You'll notice that these scales have been developed from Paul's profile on love in 1 Corinthians 13:4-8.

Step 1—Scale 1: An Exercise for Wives

Circle the number you feel best indicates the degree of agape love you exhibit toward your husband.

Degree of Love

1. My patience toward my husband   1 2 3 4 5 6 7 8 9 10
2. My kindness toward my husband   1 2 3 4 5 6 7 8 9 10
3. My lack of envy and jealousy   1 2 3 4 5 6 7 8 9 10
4. My lack of boasting (putting my husband down)   1 2 3 4 5 6 7 8 9 10
5. My lack of pride (competing with my husband)   1 2 3 4 5 6 7 8 9 10
6. My lack of rudeness   1 2 3 4 5 6 7 8 9 10
7. My lack of self-seeking (selfish behavior)   1 2 3 4 5 6 7 8 9 10
8. My not being easily angered   1 2 3 4 5 6 7 8 9 10
9. My not keeping a record of wrongs   1 2 3 4 5 6 7 8 9 10
10. My not delighting in evil (insisting that my husband participate in sinful actions)   1 2 3 4 5 6 7 8 9 10
11. My rejoicing in the truth (in doing God's will)   1 2 3 4 5 6 7 8 9 10
12. Protecting my husband   1 2 3 4 5 6 7 8 9 10
13. Trusting my husband   1 2 3 4 5 6 7 8 9 10
14. Seeing the best in my husband   1 2 3 4 5 6 7 8 9 10
15. Persevering in doing what is right   1 2 3 4 5 6 7 8 9 10

Step 1—Scale 1: An Exercise for Husbands

Circle the number you feel best indicates the degree of agape love you exhibit toward your wife.

Degree of Love

1. My patience toward my wife   1 2 3 4 5 6 7 8 9 10
2. My kindness toward my wife   1 2 3 4 5 6 7 8 9 10
3. My lack of envy and jealousy   1 2 3 4 5 6 7 8 9 10
4. My lack of boasting (putting my wife down)   1 2 3 4 5 6 7 8 9 10
5. My lack of pride (competing with my wife)   1 2 3 4 5 6 7 8 9 10
6. My lack of rudeness   1 2 3 4 5 6 7 8 9 10
7. My lack of self-seeking (selfish behavior)   1 2 3 4 5 6 7 8 9 10
8. My not being easily angered   1 2 3 4 5 6 7 8 9 10
9. My not keeping a record of wrongs   1 2 3 4 5 6 7 8 9 10
10. My not delighting in evil (insisting that my wife participate in sinful actions)   1 2 3 4 5 6 7 8 9 10
11. My rejoicing in the truth (in doing God's will)   1 2 3 4 5 6 7 8 9 10
12. Protecting my wife   1 2 3 4 5 6 7 8 9 10
13. Trusting my wife   1 2 3 4 5 6 7 8 9 10
14. Seeing the best in my wife   1 2 3 4 5 6 7 8 9 10
15. Persevering in doing what is right   1 2 3 4 5 6 7 8 9 10

Step 2—Instructions for Both Spouses

Complete the following evaluation scale on your mate (Scale 2). This scale is designed to give you an opportunity to express the degree of agape love you feel your mate expresses toward you.

Step 2—Scale 2 For Wives: About Their Husbands

Circle the number you feel describes the degree of agape love your husband expresses toward you.

Degree of Love

1. My husband's patience toward me — 1 2 3 4 5 6 7 8 9 10
2. My husband's kindness toward me — 1 2 3 4 5 6 7 8 9 10
3. His lack of envy and jealousy — 1 2 3 4 5 6 7 8 9 10
4. His lack of boasting (putting me down) — 1 2 3 4 5 6 7 8 9 10
5. His lack of pride (competing with me) — 1 2 3 4 5 6 7 8 9 10
6. His lack of rudeness — 1 2 3 4 5 6 7 8 9 10
7. His lack of self-seeking (selfish behavior) — 1 2 3 4 5 6 7 8 9 10
8. His not being easily angered — 1 2 3 4 5 6 7 8 9 10
9. His not keeping a record of wrongs — 1 2 3 4 5 6 7 8 9 10
10. His not delighting in evil (insisting that I participate in sinful actions) — 1 2 3 4 5 6 7 8 9 10
11. His rejoicing in the truth (in doing God's will) — 1 2 3 4 5 6 7 8 9 10
12. His protecting me — 1 2 3 4 5 6 7 8 9 10
13. His trusting me — 1 2 3 4 5 6 7 8 9 10
14. His seeing the best in me — 1 2 3 4 5 6 7 8 9 10
15. His persevering in doing what is right — 1 2 3 4 5 6 7 8 9 10

Step 2—Scale 2 For Husbands: About Their Wives

Circle the number you feel describes the degree of agape love your wife expresses to you.

Degree of Love

1. My wife's patience toward me   1 2 3 4 5 6 7 8 9 10

2. My wife's kindness toward me   1 2 3 4 5 6 7 8 9 10

3. Her lack of envy and jealousy   1 2 3 4 5 6 7 8 9 10

4. Her lack of boasting (putting me down)   1 2 3 4 5 6 7 8 9 10

5. Her lack of pride (competing with me)   1 2 3 4 5 6 7 8 9 10

6. Her lack of rudeness   1 2 3 4 5 6 7 8 9 10

7. Her lack of self-seeking (selfish behavior)   1 2 3 4 5 6 7 8 9 10

8. Her not being easily angered   1 2 3 4 5 6 7 8 9 10

9. Her not keeping a record of wrongs   1 2 3 4 5 6 7 8 9 10

10. Her not delighting in evil (insisting that I participate in sinful actions)   1 2 3 4 5 6 7 8 9 10

11. Her rejoicing in the truth (in doing God's will)   1 2 3 4 5 6 7 8 9 10

12. Her protecting me   1 2 3 4 5 6 7 8 9 10

13. Her trusting me   1 2 3 4 5 6 7 8 9 10

14. Her seeing the best in me   1 2 3 4 5 6 7 8 9 10

15. Her persevering in doing what is right   1 2 3 4 5 6 7 8 9 10

Step 3—Instructions for Both Spouses

Compare your responses in Scales 1 and 2 by filling out the following comparative evaluation worksheets.

Step 3—Scale 3: Worksheet for Wives

(Wife's Scale Compared with Husband's Evaluation)

As a wife, record your personal evaluation numbers (Scale 1) and your husband's evaluation of you (Scale 2). Put a plus (+) beside each item to indicate if your husband rates you higher than you do. Place a minus (-) beside each item to indicate if your husband rates you lower than you do.

		Scale 1 My Personal Evaluation	Scale 2 My Husband's Evaluation of me
__	1. Degree of patience	_____	_____
__	2. Degree of kindness	_____	_____
__	3. Lack of envy and jealousy	_____	_____
__	4. Lack of boasting	_____	_____
__	5. Lack of pride	_____	_____
__	6. Lack of rudeness	_____	_____
__	7. Lack of self-seeking	_____	_____
__	8. Not easily angered	_____	_____
__	9. Not keeping a record of wrongs	_____	_____
__	10. Not delighting in evil	_____	_____
__	11. Rejoicing in the truth	_____	_____
__	12. Degree of protection	_____	_____
__	13. Degree of trust	_____	_____
__	14. Seeing the best	_____	_____
__	15. Persevering in doing what is right	_____	_____

Step 3—Scale 3: Worksheet for Husbands

(Husband's Scale Compared with Wife's Evaluation)

As a husband, record your personal evaluation numbers (Scale 1) and your wife's evaluation of you (Scale 2). Put a plus (+) beside each item to indicate if your wife rates you higher than you do. Place a minus (-) beside each item to indicate if your wife rates you lower than you do.

	Scale 1 My Personal Evaluation	Scale 2 My Wife's Evaluation of me
__ 1. Degree of patience	_____	_____
__ 2. Degree of kindness	_____	_____
__ 3. Lack of envy and jealousy	_____	_____
__ 4. Lack of boasting	_____	_____
__ 5. Lack of pride	_____	_____
__ 6. Lack of rudeness	_____	_____
__ 7. Lack of self-seeking	_____	_____
__ 8. Not easily angered	_____	_____
__ 9. Not keeping a record of wrongs	_____	_____
__ 10. Not delighting in evil	_____	_____
__ 11. Rejoicing in the truth	_____	_____
__ 12. Degree of protection	_____	_____
__ 13. Degree of trust	_____	_____
__ 14. Seeing the best	_____	_____
__ 15. Persevering in doing what is right	_____	_____

Step 4—Instructions for Both Spouses

You are ready now to isolate areas of strength as well as areas for improvement.

First, look for discrepancies between your "personal evaluation of yourself" and your "mate's evaluation of you." The items beside which you placed a minus (-) will indicate the areas of discrepancies where you will need to concentrate. Plus (+) items indicate that you are harder on yourself than your mate is. Be encouraged!

Note: To be a significant discrepancy, there should be two or more points difference. For example, if your mate circled number 5 regarding your "degree of patience" and you gave yourself a 6, consider this equal. However, if there's a two-point spread, consider this an area to look at carefully. Obviously, the greater the spread, the greater the significance in difference and the more attention you should give that particular item.

Second, in isolating areas of need, look for those items that are circled from 1 to 6. Consider 7 or above a very good score. However, even if your scores do range mostly at 7 or above, you still have room for significant improvement. But realize that, if you rate this high with each other, you are making great progress in learning to love.

Step 5—Instructions for Both Spouses

After evaluating your responses on Scales 1, 2 and 3, each of you should answer the questions on the following "Worksheet for Wives" and "Worksheet for Husbands."

Step 5—Worksheet for Wives

Answer as many of these questions on your own as possible. Then consult your husband to help you answer those you find difficult to answer alone.

1. What manifestations of love, as outlined in 1 Corinthians 13, do I appreciate most about my husband?

2. What areas are there where I evidently feel I am more loving toward my husband than I really am? Explain why this may be true.

3. What weaknesses in my husband cause me the most difficulty in my marriage?

4. In what areas do my own weaknesses evidently accentuate my husband's weaknesses?

5. In what areas do my strengths evidently help my husband overcome his weaknesses?

Step 5—Worksheet for Husbands

Answer as many of these questions on your own as possible. Then consult your wife to help you answer those you find difficult to answer alone.

1. What manifestations of love, as outlined in 1 Corinthians 13, do I appreciate most about my wife?

2. What areas are there where I evidently feel I am more loving toward my wife than I really am? Explain why this may be true.

3. What weaknesses in my wife cause me the most difficulty in my marriage?

4. In what areas do my own weaknesses evidently accentuate my wife's weaknesses?

5. In what areas do my strengths evidently help my wife overcome her weaknesses?

Step 6—Instructions for Both Spouses

Share what you've written on your worksheets with your mate either silently by letting him or her read what you have written or by sharing it aloud.

Note: Decide together which approach you would rather use.

Step 7—Instructions for Both Spouses

After discussing together what you can do to help each other improve in your areas of weakness, write out specific goals on the sheets that follow.

Step 7—For Wives: Goals for Becoming More Loving Toward My Husband

After sharing your observations with each other from your worksheets, think of specific situations where you find it difficult to reflect certain aspects of love toward your husband. Then, write out goals you plan to achieve in those particular situations.

Example: You may find it difficult to be patient toward your husband when you are tired. Your goal might read:

"I am planning to get more rest during the day so that, when my husband comes home, I'll be more patient toward him."

1.

2.

3.

(over)

Goals for Helping My Husband Become More Loving Toward Me

Example: You may notice that your husband becomes impatient when he is tired. Your goal might read:
   "I am planning to put fewer demands on my husband when I know he is tired."

1.

2.

3

Step 7—For Husbands: Goals for Becoming More Loving Toward My Wife

After sharing your observations with each other from your worksheets, think of specific situations where you find it difficult to reflect certain aspects of love toward your wife. Then write out goals you plan to achieve in those particular situations.

Example: You may find it difficult to be patient toward your wife when you are tired. Your goal might read:

"Since my work schedule is predetermined and results in tiredness when I come home—causing me to be impatient with my wife—I will discuss my problem with her so she will understand my predicament. I will also plan time in my overall schedule to be with her socially when I am well-rested and my emotional energy is not depleted."

1.

2.

3

(over)

Goals for Helping My Wife Become More Loving Toward Me

Example: You may notice that your wife becomes impatient when she is tired. Your goal might read:
   "I will plan to put fewer demands on my wife when I know she is tired. I will also communicate to her that I understand how she feels since I also become impatient when I am tired."

1.

2.

3

Step 8—Instructions for Both Spouses

As a couple, use Paul's prayer for the Romans, applying it to your own relationship:

> May our love be without hypocrisy. May we abhor what is evil and cling to what is good. May we be devoted to one another in brotherly love, giving preference to one another in honor (Rom. 12:9,10 paraphrase).

Note

1. Mort Katz, *Marriage Survival Kit* (Rockville Centre, NY: Farnsworth Publishing Company, Inc., 1974), p. 44.

6
UNDERSTANDING
EACH OTHER

All human beings are unique—primarily because we are made in God's image. But, beyond that, each of us is an individual. And, as individuals, we have unique needs, concerns, interests, talents and potentialities.

But there is yet another difference. We are uniquely male and female. Though both men and women reflect many similarities, we are indeed different in certain respects. And, in order to meet one another's needs, we must understand one another, not only as individual human beings, but as men and women.

Understanding Your Wife

The apostle Peter spoke directly to this issue in his first letter when he exhorted: "You husbands likewise, live with your wives in an *understanding way*" (1 Pet. 3:7) or, literally, live with your wives "according to knowledge." From a practical point of view, Peter was saying that husbands are responsible before God to become students of their wives, to make a special effort to understand their particular uniqueness. This involves not only understanding them as individuals because they are human beings, but also as special people. Peter goes on to make this clear.

Your Wife Is a Woman

Live with your wife in an understanding way, continued Peter, "since she is a *woman*."

Today, some people are attempting to eliminate unique distinctions between men and women. This is not only biblically unsound, but cannot be demonstrated pragmatically. True, there have been differentiations over the years that are absolutely absurd, unfair and unfounded. But certain distinctions are there nevertheless, even though men, particularly, have widened the gap far beyond reality. Though Adam first recognized Eve's humanness because of her similarities to him, he then discovered that she was uniquely different from him. She was a woman (see Gen. 2:23).

Your Wife Is a Weaker Vessel

Peter also stated something in this verse of Scripture that causes some women to act defensively. "Live with your wives in an understanding way," wrote Peter, "as with a *weaker vessel*" (1 Pet. 3:7).

One day I was lecturing on this subject in a well-known institution of higher learning. A bright young woman put up her hand and asked, "Are you sure this is not some kind of translation error? Does the original language in the New Testament actually read 'a weaker vessel'?"

My answer had to be first no, and then yes. No, this is not a translation error. Yes, it does mean a "weaker vessel" in the original New Testament text. In other words, this is what Peter actually said.

The problem is that some Bible interpreters have made Peter say far more than he meant. In fact, one very uninformed and prejudiced male once interpreted this phrase to mean that women are weak in point of sex, the constitution of their body, mind and judgment, art, aptitude and wisdom in the conduct of affairs.

That interpretation is embarrassing. Unfortunately, some men actually believe this. But it is particularly true among men in non-Christian religions. For example, some Muslims actually believe that a woman does not have a soul. But how tragic when people who claim to believe the Bible teach such nonsense. Women often excel men in mental abilities, psychological and physical endurance (women live longer), and in both scientific and artistic achievements.

What, then, does Peter actually mean? The answer is really quite simple. The apostle is referring to the degree of physical strength that women normally have when compared with men. Though there are exceptions, men by creation have more brute strength. This is easily observable in certain kinds of athletic activities today. Though women can often compete equally and even exceed men in some sports—such as skiing and skating—you seldom see women able to hold their own against men in the more physically demanding sports such as basketball, football and hockey. Women, in this respect, are the weaker vessels.

Our daughter, Robyn, is a runner, having competed in several marathons. One day we saw her do an eight-mile run with over 10,000 other people. She did very well—which she usually does. But I noticed in the paper the next day that the 50th man to cross the finish line was one second ahead of the first woman to cross the line. Why? Man is by nature stronger physically. This is primarily what Peter had in mind when he identified a wife as a weaker vessel.

Your Wife Is a Sexual Partner
Some believe that the most basic and literal meaning of

this verse has to do with the weaker vessel in sexual intercourse. In other words, when Peter wrote, *"Live with* [dwell together with] your wives in an understanding way," he may have been first and foremost referring to the sexual relationship. Thus Peter would be saying, "Husbands, when you have sexual relations with your wives, do so with understanding and sensitivity, remembering that she, as a woman, is not as strong as you are."

Personally, I would not restrict what Peter had in mind to this interpretation, though this kind of understanding is certainly inherent in what he says. Any Christian husband who is insensitive to his wife's physical capabilities in this most intimate area of life is indeed selfish and not understanding. And, of course, there's a great deal of variation among individual women in terms of actual physical strength and sexual responsiveness. This, too, must be considered if a Christian husband is to obey God and live with his wife in an understanding way.

But just as important, if not more so, as understanding a woman's physical makeup is understanding her emotional needs. This certainly must be included in Peter's injunction. I say this because observations verify the importance of this again and again. We have seen many situations where a wife has been treated insensitively over a period of time, usually for several years. In turn, she has attempted to tolerate the situation as best she could. Finally, however, her feelings of love die and become either numb or negative. In some instances, she suddenly turns and walks away from the marriage, leaving her husband dumbfounded. When he asks her why, he discovers for the first time that she has been feeling hurt and resentful for years because of his insensitivity to her feelings. "Why didn't you tell me?" he asks.

"I tried to," she replies, "but you wouldn't listen. Now it's too late."

Unfortunately, when a woman really believes it's too late, it's very difficult to change her mind.

Obviously, most of these situations are two-way problems. The fault lies on both sides. But it does underscore why a husband must understand his wife.

Understanding Your Husband

Though Peter does not specifically tell wives to live with their husbands in an understanding way, it is definitely implied in what he does say.

In chapter 3 verses 1-6, Peter specifically deals with a Christian wife's relationship to a non-Christian husband. This was a particular problem among those to whom Peter was writing. Evidently a number of women were becoming followers of Christ, whereas their pagan husbands were not responding to the message of Christianity. Peter exhorted these women to be submissive to these men—that is, not to resist or rebel against them. Furthermore, they were to demonstrate the realities of Christianity primarily with their life-styles rather than with theological statements. They were definitely to be loyal to these men sexually, though some certainly were tempted to become involved with Christian men who would be more understanding and sensitive. And, rather than emphasizing external adornment, they were to demonstrate true inner qualities—"a gentle and quiet spirit."

Recognizing his weakness
Peter's specific instructions to these women involve behavior on their part that reflects keen insight into the unique male personality. Ironically, men have often been classified as being superior to women. In this passage, Peter implies that, in at least one area of life, men seem to be inferior, particularly in terms of ego strength.

The male ego is a very sensitive dimension in every man. Though it often reflects strength, it is frequently a cover-up for weakness and feelings of insecurity. A woman who either attacks a male ego or ignores it is only aggravating the problem. She certainly is not living with her husband in an understanding way.

Peter, it seems, was, by implication at least, treating this aspect of the male personality. He exhorted these women to be sensitive to this unique problem. Just as a husband is to be sensitive to a woman's lack of physical strength, so a woman is to be sensitive to a man's lack of ego strength.

This observation has been verified again and again in our own counseling experiences with couples who are having difficulty in their relationship. A woman who attacks or ignores a man's ego needs can, in some instances, actually incapacitate him. For example, he may not be able to perform sexually; or if he can perform, he is not able to do so sensitively and compassionately. Furthermore, he may become withdrawn and uncommunicative; or he may become angry or resentful, which interferes with his ability to be emotionally sensitive and understanding.

In these situations, a man is also extremely vulnerable. He is easily tempted into an extramarital affair by a woman who does understand his ego needs. Ironically, most successful prostitutes are masters at understanding men in this area of their lives. And this also explains why some men, even Christian men, will give up everything—a good Christian woman, children, a home, position and finances—to live with another woman. At that moment in his life, more important to him than anything else in the whole world, even his Christianity, is that his ego needs be met. This is tragic, but true. We've seen it happen to some of our own acquaintances.

Dealing with his weakness
A vital relationship with Jesus Christ can, of course, change a man. But conversion to Christianity and a desire to live according to God's will does not automati-

cally eliminate the problem every man has with his fleshly nature, which he inherited from Adam. This was why Peter exhorted Christian husbands to live with their wives in an understanding way and to grant them "honor as a fellow-heir of the grace of life" (1 Pet. 3:7).

Every man needs a woman who understands his ego needs. And every woman needs a man who understands her uniqueness as a woman.

But, as with every relationship in life, this is a two-way street. Every man needs a woman who understands his ego needs. And every woman needs a man who understands her uniqueness as a woman. And, through mutual understanding, they can grow together, meeting each other's needs, whatever those needs might be.

Peter concluded his instructions to people in general and to husbands and wives in particular by saying:

> *To sum up, let all be harmonious, sympathetic, brotherly, kind-hearted, and humble in spirit; not returning evil for evil, or insult for insult, but giving a blessing instead; for you were called for the very purpose that you might inherit a blessing* (1 Pet. 3:8,9).

An Exercise in Developing Feeling Love

We have already considered the three dimensions of love that are discussed and illustrated in the Bible (see fig. 1). Generally speaking, agape love involves doing what is right and best for someone, even if it involves negative feelings. Phileo love often refers to the dimension of love that involves responding to someone's needs affectionately and with positive emotions. Erao love involves sexual response.

Though there are many instances when we must demonstrate love at the action level even when we don't feel like it (that is, if a marriage is to work), it is not God's will that our lives together as husbands and wives be characterized primarily by negative feelings. Rather, we are to enjoy each other, not merely endure a painful relationship.

Though there are many instances when we must demonstrate love at the action level even when we don't feel like it, it is not God's will that our lives together as husbands and wives be characterized primarily by negative feelings.

Probably 99 percent of all men and women in our culture enter marriage with positive feelings. Unfortunately, these feelings are often physically oriented, rather than reflecting a love that is comprehensive and based on mature understanding and feelings. Fortunately, many of these couples soon learn to love each other at a deeper level. On the other hand, what began as a strong physical attraction, in some instances, subsides rather quickly or turns to feelings of resentment and anger.

How can a marriage, no matter at what level it began in terms of love, grow and mature at the feeling level? The answer to this question is to live together in an understanding way. It is only as we come to know each other emotionally that we can minister to each other emotionally. This involves learning to communicate at the feeling level. The following evaluation exercises are designed to help you accomplish that goal.

Step 1—Instructions for Both Spouses

It is important that you, as a couple, learn how to share and exchange feelings. To achieve this goal, spend as much time as necessary separately making observations on the following worksheets.

Step 1—An Exercise in Developing Feeling Love

A Worksheet for Wives

1. Write down the areas where you believe you communicate well with your husband and he communicates well with you. That is, you discuss these matters together and reach conclusions objectively, clearly, and with understanding and sensitivity.

2. Write down the areas where you have difficulty communicating with your husband.

3. Write down any additional areas where you communicate with your husband very superficially or not at all.

Step 1—An Exercise in Developing Feeling Love

A Worksheet for Husbands

1. Write down the areas where you believe you communicate well with your wife and she communicates well with you. That is, you discuss these matters together and reach conclusions objectively, clearly, and with understanding and sensitivity.

2. Write down the areas where you have difficulty communicating with your wife.

3. Write down any additional areas where you communicate with your wife very superficially or not at all.

Step 2—Instructions for Both Spouses

Now that you have recorded your responses to the questions on your worksheets, share your answers with each other by reading what your mate has written. Then discuss your answers beginning with question 1. Then both of you should move to question 2, and finally to question 3. Note differences in opinion as well as agreement. Try to discover why the differences exist.

Step 3—Instructions for Both Spouses

Analyze your communication style with your mate on the following scales.

Step 3—Scale 1 For Wives: Analyzing Your Communication Style

Put a check (✔) beside the statement that best describes your communication style with your husband.

When you state your opinions or desires to your husband . . .

Do you say:	Or	Do you say:
___ Pick up your . . .		___ Would you please be kind enough to . . . ?
___ Why don't you . . . ?		___ Have you thought about trying . . . ?
___ There must be a better way to do that.		___ Perhaps you would do better if you . . .
___ You sure know how to hurt me.		___ I'm glad you let me know exactly how you feel, even though it's painful for me.
___ Don't pry so much.		___ I'm glad you feel free to ask that kind of question.
___ Thanks for doing . . .		___ You certainly did a good job on that.
___ I'm glad you finally got that . . . done.		___ I admire the way you use your time to complete jobs like that.
___ I'm glad you finally . . .		___ It was very thoughtful of you to . . .
___ I'm glad we have finally gone out to dinner.		___ I enjoyed eating out so much. Thanks for taking me there.

Remember: You are automatically a negative communicator if you don't say anything when you could express appreciation in a positive manner.

Step 3—Scale 1 For Husbands: Analyzing Your Communication Style

Put a check (✔) beside the statement that best describes your communication style with your wife.

When you state your opinions or desires to your husband . . .

Do you say:	Or	Do you say:
___ Why don't you . . . ?		___ Have you thought about trying . . . ?
___ Let's go . . .		___ How would you feel about going . . . ?
___ There must be a better way to do that.		___ Perhaps you would do better if you . . .
___ You sure know how to hurt me.		___ I'm glad you let me know exactly how you feel, even though it's painful for me.
___ Don't pry so much.		___ I'm glad you feel free to ask that kind of question.
___ Thanks for doing . . .		___ You certainly did a good job on that.
___ I'm glad you finally got that . . . done.		___ I admire the way you use your time to complete jobs like that.
___ I'm glad you finally . . .		___ It was very thoughtful of you to . . .
___ Thanks for the meal.		___ You're a wonderful cook. Dinner was delicious.

Remember: You are automatically a negative communicator if you don't say anything when you could express appreciation in a positive manner.

Step 4—Instructions for Both Spouses

Now that each of you has completed the exercises for evaluating your own communication style with your mate, evaluate your mate's communication style by completing Scale 2, which follows.

Step 4—Scale 2: Evaluating Your Husband's Communication Style

Put a check (✔) beside the statement that best describes your husband's communication style with you.

When your husband states his opinions or desires . . .

He says: Or   **He says:**

_____ Why don't you . . . ?

_____ Have you thought about trying . . . ?

_____ Let's go . . .

_____ How would you feel about going . . . ?

_____ There must be a better way to do that.

_____ Perhaps you would do better if you . . .

_____ You sure know how to hurt me.

_____ I'm glad you let me know exactly how you feel, even though it's painful for me.

_____ Don't pry so much.

_____ I'm glad you feel free to ask that kind of question.

_____ Thanks for doing . . .

_____ You certainly did a good job on that.

_____ I'm glad you finally got that . . . done.

_____ I admire the way you use your time to complete jobs like that.

_____ I'm glad you finally . . .

_____ It was very thoughtful of you to . . .

_____ Thanks for the meal.

_____ You're a wonderful cook. Dinner was delicious.

Step 4—Scale 2: Evaluating Your Wife's Communication Style

Put a check (✔) beside the statement that best describes your wife's communication style with you.

When your wife states her opinions or desires . . .

She says: Or   **She says:**

_____ Pick up your . . .

_____ Would you please be kind enough to . . . ?

_____ Why don't you . . . ?

_____ Have you thought about trying . . . ?

_____ There must be a better way to do that.

_____ Perhaps you would do better if you . . .

_____ You sure know how to hurt me.

_____ I'm glad you let me know exactly how you feel, even though it's painful for me.

_____ Don't pry so much.

_____ I'm glad you feel free to ask that kind of question.

_____ Thanks for doing . . .

_____ You certainly did a good job on that.

_____ I'm glad you finally got that . . . done.

_____ I admire the way you use your time to complete jobs like that.

_____ I'm glad you finally . . .

_____ It was very thoughtful of you to . . .

_____ I'm glad we have finally gone out to dinner.

_____ I enjoyed eating out so much. Thanks for taking me there.

Step 5—Instructions for Both Spouses

Compare *your* evaluation of your own communication style with your mate's evaluation of your communication style. Do so by completing the following comparative worksheets,
Scale 3.

Step 5—Scale 3: Wife's Scale Compared with Husband's Evaluation

Record in the appropriate spaces the answers (✔) you gave in Scale 1 of Step 2 and the answers your husband gave in Scale 2 of Step 4 on your communication style.

When I state my opinions or desires to my husband . . .

		I say:	Or			I say:
Scale 1 Personal Evalua- tion	Scale 2 Husband's Evalua- tion			Scale 1 Personal Evalua- tion	Scale 2 Husband's Evalua- tion	
—	—	Pick up your . . .		—	—	Would you please be kind enough to . . . ?
—	—	Why don't you . . . ?		—	—	Have you thought about trying . . . ?
—	—	There must be a better way to do that.		—	—	Perhaps you would do bet- ter if you . . .
—	—	You sure know how to hurt me.		—	—	I'm glad you let me know exactly how you feel, even though it's painful for me.
—	—	Don't pry so much.		—	—	I'm glad you feel free to ask that kind of question.

(over)

__ __ Thanks for doing . . .

__ __ I'm glad you finally got that . . . done.

__ __ I'm glad you finally . . .

__ __ I'm glad we have finally gone out to dinner.

__ __ You certainly did a good job on that.

__ __ I admire the way you use your time to complete jobs like that.

__ __ It was very thoughtful of you to . . .

__ __ I enjoyed eating out so much. Thanks for taking me there.

Step 5—Scale 3: Husband's Scale Compared with Wife's Evaluation

Record in the appropriate spaces the answers (✔) you gave in Scale 1 of Step 2 and the answers your wife gave in Scale 2 of Step 4 on your communication style.

When I state my opinions or desires to my wife . . .

	I say:	Or		I say:
Scale 1 Personal Evalua- tion	Scale 2 Wife's Evalua- tion		Scale 1 Personal Evalua- tion	Scale 2 Wife's Evalua- tion
__ __	Why don't you . . . ?		__ __	Have you thought about trying . . . ?
__ __	There must be a better way to do that.		__ __	Perhaps you would do bet- ter if you . . .
__ __	You sure know how to hurt me.		__ __	I'm glad you let me know exactly how you feel, even though it's painful for me.
__ __	Don't pry so much.		__ __	I'm glad you feel free to ask that kind of question.
__ __	Thanks for doing . . .		__ __	You certainly did a good job on that.

(over)

— — I'm glad you finally got that . . . done.

— — I admire the way you use your time to complete jobs like that.

— — I'm glad you finally . . .

— — It was very thoughtful of you to . . .

— — Thanks for the meal.

— — You're a wonderful cook. Dinner was delicious.

Step 6—Instructions for Both Spouses

Use the comparative worksheets you have just completed to analyze how you view your own communication style compared with how your mate views your communication style. Isolate areas of agreement and disagreement. Discuss why this disagreement exists and how you can become more sensitive and understanding in your communication with each other.

Step 7—Instructions for Both Spouses

Now that you've completed the preceding steps, utilize the following exercises to help you and your spouse share and express feelings. Follow through on this exercise for at least five days. You may write in your answers and let your mate read your responses out loud if you have difficulty verbalizing them. If necessary, consult the list of positive and negative emotions that follow in order to use these exercises:

Positive Feelings	Negative Feelings
Pleased	Anxious
Understanding	Fear
Hopeful	Lonely
Tenderness	Uncertainty
Proud	Insecure
Closeness	Confusion
Excited	Sad
Happiness	Rejection
Contented	Angry
Confident	Bored
Acceptance	Helplessness
Grateful	Scared
Affectionate	Frustrated
Sexual arousal	Frigidity
Eager	Foolish
Elated	Confused
Calm	Apathetic

Step 7—For Wives: A Daily Exercise in Learning to Communicate at the Feeling Level

Each day for the next five days, using the following statements, let your husband express the emotion or emotions he is feeling. If necessary, he can consult the preceding list of positive and negative emotions. Initially, he may wish to write in his answers and allow you to read his responses. Writing down your feelings is a good way to begin the process of communication.

Day 1

Wife·   What are you feeling inside right now, _____
_____?
            (husband's name)

Husband: I am feeling _____.
Wife: Can you describe your feelings more specifically?

Husband: I feel _____ about
_____.

Wife: Do I hear you saying that you are feeling ___
_____ about _____?
            (Repeat what you hear your husband saying.)

Husband: Yes (or no). (Wife, if your husband answers no, ask him to repeat how he feels. Then repeat what you hear him saying until he feels you have indeed heard him clearly.)

Wife: Thanks for sharing your feelings with me.

Husband: Thank you for listening to my feelings. (Wife, if the feelings your husband is experiencing are negative, ask, "What can I do to help you feel better?")

Husband: You can help me feel better by _____
_____
_____
_____
_____
_____

Day 2

Wife: What are you feeling inside right now, _____

_____?
           (husband's name)

Husband: I am feeling _____.

Wife: Can you describe your feelings more specifically?

Husband: I feel _____ about

_____.

Wife: Do I hear you saying that you are feeling ____

_____ about _____?
           (Repeat what you hear your husband saying.)

Husband: Yes (or no). (Wife, if your husband answers no, ask him to repeat how he feels. Then repeat what you hear him saying until he feels you have indeed heard him clearly.)

Wife: Thanks for sharing your feelings with me.

Husband: Thank you for listening to my feelings. (Wife, if the feelings your husband is experiencing are negative, ask, "What can I do to help you feel better?")

Husband: You can help me feel better by _____

_____

_____

_____

_____

_____

Day 3

Wife: What are you feeling inside right now, ____

_____?

(husband's name)

Husband: I am feeling _____.

Wife: Can you describe your feelings more specifically?

Husband: I feel _____ about

_____.

Wife: Do I hear you saying that you are feeling ___

_____ about _____?

(Repeat what you hear your husband saying.)

Husband: Yes (or no). (Wife, if your husband answers
no, ask him to repeat how he feels. Then
repeat what you hear him saying until he feels
you have indeed heard him clearly.)

Wife: Thanks for sharing your feelings with me.

Husband: Thank you for listening to my feelings. (Wife, if
the feelings your husband is experiencing are
negative, ask, "What can I do to help you feel
better?")

Husband: You can help me feel better by _____

_____

_____

_____

_____

Day 4

Wife: What are you feeling inside right now, _____

_____?

(husband's name)

Husband: I am feeling _____.

Wife: Can you describe your feelings more specifically?

Husband: I feel _____ about

_____.

Wife: Do I hear you saying that you are feeling ____

_____ about _____?

(Repeat what you hear your husband saying.)

Husband: Yes (or no). (Wife, if your husband answers no, ask him to repeat how he feels. Then repeat what you hear him saying until he feels you have indeed heard him clearly.)

Wife: Thanks for sharing your feelings with me.

Husband: Thank you for listening to my feelings. (Wife, if the feelings your husband is experiencing are negative, ask, "What can I do to help you feel better?")

Husband: You can help me feel better by _____

_____

_____

_____

_____

_____

Day 5

Wife: What are you feeling inside right now, _____

_____?

(husband's name)

Husband: I am feeling _____.

Wife: Can you describe your feelings more specifically?

Husband: I feel _____ about

_____.

Wife: Do I hear you saying that you are feeling _____

_____ about _____?

(Repeat what you hear your husband saying.)

Husband: Yes (or no). (Wife, if your husband answers no, ask him to repeat how he feels. Then repeat what you hear him saying until he feels you have indeed heard him clearly.)

Wife: Thanks for sharing your feelings with me.

Husband: Thank you for listening to my feelings. (Wife, if the feelings your husband is experiencing are negative, ask, "What can I do to help you feel better?")

Husband: You can help me feel better by _____

_____

_____

_____

_____

_____

Step 7—For Husbands: A Daily Exercise in Learning to Communicate at the Feeling Level

Each day for the next five days, using the following statements, let your wife express the emotion or emotions she is feeling. If necessary, she can consult the list of positive and negative emotions listed at the beginning of this Step 7. Initially she may wish to write in her answers and allow you to read her responses. Writing down your feelings is a good way to begin the process of communication.

Day 1

Husband: What are you feeling inside right now, _____
_____?
(wife's name)

Wife: I am feeling _____.

Husband: Can you describe your feelings more specifically?

Wife: I feel _____ about
_____.

Husband: Do I hear you saying that you are feeling ___
_____ about _____?
(Repeat what you hear your wife saying.)

Wife: Yes (or no). (Husband, if your wife answers
no, ask her to repeat how she feels. Then
repeat what you hear her saying until she
feels you have indeed heard her clearly.)

Husband: Thanks for sharing your feelings with me.

Wife: Thank you for listening to my feelings. (Husband, if the feelings your wife is experiencing
are negative, ask, "What can I do to help you
feel better?")

Wife: You can help me feel better by _____
_____
_____
_____
_____
_____

Day 2

Husband: What are you feeling inside right now, _____
_____?
(wife's name)

Wife: I am feeling _____.

Husband: Can you describe your feelings more specifically?

Wife: I feel _____ about
_____.

Husband: Do I hear you saying that you are feeling ___
_____ about _____?
(Repeat what you hear your wife saying.)

Wife: Yes (or no). (Husband, if your wife answers
no, ask her to repeat how she feels. Then
repeat what you hear her saying until she
feels you have indeed heard her clearly.)

Husband: Thanks for sharing your feelings with me.

Wife: Thank you for listening to my feelings. (Husband, if the feelings your wife is experiencing
are negative, ask, "What can I do to help you
feel better?")

Wife: You can help me feel better by _____
_____
_____
_____
_____

Day 3

Husband: What are you feeling inside right now, _____
_____?
          (wife's name)

Wife: I am feeling _____.

Husband: Can you describe your feelings more specifically?

Wife: I feel _____ about
_____.

Husband: Do I hear you saying that you are feeling ___
_____ about _____?
(Repeat what you hear your wife saying.)

Wife: Yes (or no). (Husband, if your wife answers no, ask her to repeat how she feels. Then repeat what you hear her saying until she feels you have indeed heard her clearly.)

Husband: Thanks for sharing your feelings with me.

Wife: Thank you for listening to my feelings. (Husband, if the feelings your wife is experiencing are negative, ask, "What can I do to help you feel better?")

Wife: You can help me feel better by _____
_____
_____
_____
_____
_____

Day 4

Husband: What are you feeling inside right now, _____
_____?
(wife's name)

Wife: I am feeling _____.

Husband: Can you describe your feelings more specifically?

Wife: I feel _____ about
_____.

Husband: Do I hear you saying that you are feeling ___
_____ about _____?
(Repeat what you hear your wife saying.)

Wife: Yes (or no). (Husband, if your wife answers no, ask her to repeat how she feels. Then repeat what you hear her saying until she feels you have indeed heard her clearly.)

Husband: Thanks for sharing your feelings with me.

Wife: Thank you for listening to my feelings. (Husband, if the feelings your wife is experiencing are negative, ask, "What can I do to help you feel better?")

Wife: You can help me feel better by _____
_____
_____
_____
_____

Day 5

Husband: What are you feeling inside right now, _____
_____?
(wife's name)

Wife: I am feeling _____.

Husband: Can you describe your feelings more specifically?

Wife: I feel _____ about
_____.

Husband: Do I hear you saying that you are feeling ___
_____ about _____?
(Repeat what you hear your wife saying.)

Wife: Yes (or no). (Husband, if your wife answers no, ask her to repeat how she feels. Then repeat what you hear her saying until she feels you have indeed heard her clearly.)

Husband: Thanks for sharing your feelings with me.

Wife: Thank you for listening to my feelings. (Husband, if the feelings your wife is experiencing are negative, ask, "What can I do to help you feel better?")

Wife: You can help me feel better by _____
_____
_____
_____
_____
_____

Step 8—Instructions for Both Spouses

As a couple, use Paul's words to the Philippians as a prayer, applying it to your relationship.

> May we do nothing from selfishness or empty conceit, but with humility of mind let each of us regard one another as more important than himself. May we not merely look out for our own personal interests, but also for the interests of the other.
> (Phil. 2:3, 4 paraphrase)

7

MEETING EACH OTHER'S SEXUAL NEEDS

The Bible clearly and forthrightly teaches that regular sexual relationships are designed by God to be a natural and normal part of marriage. The apostle Paul probably spoke more specifically in this regard than any other biblical author. In writing to the Corinthians, he stated: "Let the husband fulfill his duty to his wife, and likewise also the wife to her husband. The wife does not have authority over her own body, but the husband does; and likewise also the husband does not have authority over his own body, but the wife does. Stop depriving one another, except by agreement for a time that you may devote yourselves to prayer, and come together again lest Satan tempt you because of your lack of self-control" (1 Cor. 7:3-5).

From this passage, we can see that the Word of God is very practical in the area of sex. In essence, Paul was teaching that people do have sexual needs. Furthermore, marriage is the place for these needs to be met. And each marital partner is responsible to make sure those needs are met. If a couple decides to abstain sexually for a time, it should be agreed upon by both, but only on a temporary basis and for spiritual reasons.

Note: Paul was not correlating the absence of sex as being a means, per se, to more holiness. Rather, abstaining temporarily would simply allow more concentrated time for prayer.

When a man and woman choose to be joined together in holy matrimony, they take upon themselves a special responsibility to meet each other's sexual needs.

It is clear from Scripture that when a man and woman choose to be joined together in holy matrimony, they take upon themselves a special responsibility to meet each other's sexual needs. Paraphrasing Paul, since their bodies now belong to each other, they are not to withhold sex from each other.

We must quickly add, however, that it is important to interpret Paul's injunctions in the light of other God-given directives and principles in Scripture relating to marriage and which have already been discussed in previous chapters. To understand sexual function and to be a satisfying as well as a satisfied sexual partner is impossible:
- unless a husband and wife are in the process of becoming one emotionally and spiritually;
- unless the husband and wife have liberated themselves emotionally from their parents and established their own home;
- unless both the husband and wife are learning to love as Christ loved;
- unless they are relating to each other in a mutually submissive way;
- unless they are learning to love at both the action and feeling levels; and
- unless they are learning to understand each other, not only as male and female but as unique individuals.

Practicing God's Principles of Marriage

Only as a husband and wife practice these principles of marriage can they experience sexual fulfillment as God intended. These divine guidelines provide the foundation that causes sexual satisfaction in marriage to endure and improve. Furthermore, they also enable a husband and wife to keep subtle, selfish desires from destroying what God intended to be a mutually satisfying experience.

The principles just outlined, which form the basis of our previous chapters, can be brought into clearer focus by once again looking at a biblical definition of love (see fig. 1 in chap. 5). Most references to love in the New Testament do not refer to sexual expression, per se. Rather, most refer to agapao love—doing what is right and best for someone, even if it involves negative feelings.

Closely aligned with agapao love is phileo love—responding to someone's needs affectionately and with positive emotions, but always within the guidelines of agapao love. For the most part, it is God's will that agapao and phileo love overlap. But the Bible clearly assumes there are times when we must do things for someone because to do so is right, not because we necessarily desire to do them.

This obligation poses a problem when it comes to erao love, which involves physical and emotional involvement with another person sexually. Men, particularly and generally, cannot function sexually without erotic feelings. Unfortunately, however, a man can experience these erotic feelings purely at a selfish level and with any woman who is sexually available. Putting it simply, it is easy for a man to engage in erotic love outside the circle of biblical love (see fig. 1 in chap. 5). The history of female prostitution affirms this point.

In some respects, women have the same capability, but not as naturally as men. This is why most biblical injunctions regarding moral purity are directed at men (see Exod. 20:17; Matt. 5:28; 1 Tim. 3:2; Titus 1:6). A fact of life, generally speaking, is that men are more visually and erotically oriented when it comes to sex. They are more easily aroused, more physically oriented, and more vulnerable to sexual temptation at the erotic level.

Women, on the other hand, are more emotionally oriented. Though they are very capable of being intensely erotic, they usually respond sexually to a man who provides them with security, who understands their deep feelings, who is sensitive, tender and compassionate. Their extramarital affairs are normally precipitated because they are angry, lonesome, insecure, or generally unhappy and unfulfilled. In other words, most women are not motivated to engage in sex simply because of intense erotic drives.

Note: Men are also vulnerable when these emotional states occur. When emotional needs and physical needs are combined, they can be a lethal combination in terms of temptation. On the other hand, a man may choose to engage in extramarital sex simply because he has a physical need. This is not to say that some women may not do the same thing, but it is usually the exception, not the rule.

What does all of this mean in a marriage where both the husband and wife are committed to Christian values? In essence, it means that as Christians we need to understand each other. Being Christians does not change the physical and emotional makeup of men and women. All human beings experience the same basic needs. Knowing Jesus Christ personally, however, can and should intensify our desire to understand each other's sexual needs and to meet those needs in God-ordained ways.

Getting to know each other sexually in a marital relationship is one of the great adventures God has designed for husbands and wives. Though creativity in this area of a couple's life must be sensitively developed within the context of both agapao (action) and phileo

---

Getting to know each other sexually in a marital relationship is one of the great adventures God has designed for husbands and wives.

(feeling) love, it nevertheless provides, in itself, a life-long challenge. Like any activity in life, sexual relationships can become routine and meaningless for any couple. The suggestions that follow are designed to help every Christian couple keep this area of life interesting, challenging and mutually satisfying.

As a Wife

Most men are quite consistent in their sexual makeup. There are exceptions, of course, but, generally, when you understand one man, you have a fairly good understanding of all men. In this sense, most wives have an advantage over their husbands in that the task of gaining understanding of a man's sexual nature is not nearly as complex as that of men trying to understand their wives.

How well do I understand my husband's sexual nature?

Following are some key insights to help you understand the average husband:

- Sexually, he is visually oriented.
- He can be sexually aroused almost instantaneously.
- His sexual drive is closely related to the ebb and flow of glandular fluids.

Note: It is virtually impossible for a sexually active man to suddenly turn off his sexual desires. His sexual drive has now become a spontaneous physiological process. Once he has become used to regular sexual emissions, prostate fluid is produced accordingly. Furthermore, any kind of visual stimulation sexually (which is rampant in our culture), activates the prostate gland and it begins to produce more fluid, creating pressure on the prostate gland, which, in turn, intensifies sexual desire.

- A man's ego is closely aligned with what his wife thinks about him sexually. For example, a man whose wife demonstrates negative attitudes toward his genitals feels intensely rejected as a total person. In a sense, this is ironic because a man is very capable of compartmentalizing sex. On the other hand, his sexual organs are intricately related to his total personality. In this sense, he does not compartmentalize.

How aware am I of my husband's sexual temptations?

- Most women who dress provocatively arouse a man sexually. Because many women in today's work-a-day world dress provocatively, the average husband—even the Christian husband—is, to a certain extent, sexually stimulated nearly every day, and by more than one woman. In today's world, this kind of sexual stimulation is virtually beyond a man's control. To be in the world and not be sexually stimulated by the world is difficult.
- Most advertising today, whether it is in the newspapers, magazines, TV or radio, is designed to get a man's attention sexually. Since we live in a media-oriented world, the average man is exposed to some kind of erotic stimulation on a regular basis.
- The degree of arousal in the average man varies,

depending on several factors. But one of the most significant factors relates to the extent of his sexual fulfillment with his wife and particularly the regularity of sexual release.

Note: A man who gives himself over to lustful behavior as a way of life is never satisfied sexually. However, even a man who attempts to abide by God's standards faces regular sexual temptations, and experiences continual sexual needs.

How understanding am I of my husband's temptations?

Some women resent their husband's sexual nature. Remember that the average Christian husband, who has his conscience tuned to the Word of God, feels guilty already regarding his weaknesses in this area of his life. To feel resentment and lack of understanding from his wife only adds to his feelings of self-condemnation and guilt. In fact, this kind of attitude often accentuates his vulnerability to temptation.

How available am I to my husband sexually?

- Because you do not feel sexual desire does not mean your husband does not.
- Demonstrating unavailability does not diminish your husband's sexual drive; in fact, it may increase it.
- When your husband reads your unavailable signals and withdraws, it does not mean he has forgotten what he feels.
- A wise wife learns how to meet her husband's sexual needs in a creative way even when it is inconvenient for her personally (during pregnancy, menstrual periods, etc.).
- When a wife prefers not to engage in sexual relations with her husband, a wise woman learns how to say no without making her husband feel rejected.

What can I do to make myself more physically attractive?

Most women do not have to undergo physical surgery to become more attractive. Remarkable changes can result from some do-it-yourself projects:
- Avoid excessive weight.
- Bathe regularly—especially before lovemaking.
- Use cosmetics effectively.
- Dress appropriately for the bedroom.

What can I do to become a more creative lover?

Most people do not become creative lovers naturally. It takes thought and practice. Following are the great inhibitors in this process:
- Negative attitudes toward sex;
- Inappropriate information;
- Lack of information;
- Thinking only of oneself.

Remember: God has designed marriage for one man and one woman. Beyond that, He does not lock us into sexual forms. The very nature of both men's and women's physical and emotional makeup makes sex one of the areas of life for the greatest opportunity for creative exploration.

What can I do to set the stage for a pleasant environment for lovemaking?

The physical environment is important to a man. An unattractive bedroom or even poor housekeeping habits generally affect a man's feelings about sex. However, also remember that the emotional environment is just as important, if not more so, than the physical environment. Nothing is more disappointing to a man than negative attitudes in a beautiful bedroom.

As a Husband

It's important to realize that individual women vary far more in their sexual makeup than the average man. On the one hand, a small percentage of women have a high degree of natural sexual desire. On the other hand, a small percentage of women have a low degree of natural sexual desire. However, the majority of women fall somewhere in the middle. The fact is that many women, if necessary, can live comfortably (from a purely physiological point of view) without engaging in intimate sexual relationships. In this sense, they differ noticeably from men, which is very difficult for most men to understand.

This does not mean that women cannot and do not enjoy sex—even those women with a low sex drive. It does mean, however, that their nature is different. If a man does not understand this, he can be very threatened. Furthermore, his expectation levels regarding his wife and himself become very unrealistic.

How well do I understand my wife's sexual nature?

Following are several things to remember about the average woman:

- Whereas men are visually oriented, women are more oriented to what they sense and feel.
- Whereas the man is normally quickly aroused (even at a distance), a woman is normally aroused gradually and in a context of understanding, sensitivity, and appropriate physical touch and stimulation.
- Whereas a man's sexual drive is correlated with the ebb and flow of his own body fluids (internal stimulation), a woman's sexual drive is correlated more significantly with external stimuli; namely, a warm, accepting and understanding relationship with her husband.

Note: Many women experience degrees of difference in their sexual response, depending on their menstrual cycle. However, the phenomenon is far different than male secretionary processes and how they affect sexual desire and arousal.

- Whereas a man's ego is closely aligned with his sexual performance, a woman's sexual performance relates more to her sense of pride and psychological need to be an adequate sexual partner.

What can I do to help my wife be more responsive sexually?

Since a woman's sexual response is usually triggered differently than a man's, careful attention should be given to the following:

- Don't expect your wife to be ready to engage in sex just because you are.
- Don't be threatened by her initial lack of desire.
- Think of ways to make sexual response more natural and easier for your wife. Following are some suggestions:

    1. Remember that sexual feelings in a woman can begin to be aroused a long time before sexual intercourse—actually, many hours before. This is often caused by sharing loving and tender feelings. This causes a woman to feel understood, secure and accepted.
    2. Demonstrate your love to your wife unconditionally and consistently. In other words, don't compartmentalize sexual activity. Make it a part of numerous expressions of love.

Note: Some men only say, "I love you" and show affection and do nice things for their wives when they are interested in sex. This is a turn-off for many women. They feel bribed and used.

3. Plan lovemaking at a time when your wife is physically and emotionally fresh.

Note: A long day with the kids in a closed environment is not very conducive to stimulating a sexual response. Be understanding about these circumstances. Plan ways to circumvent these problems.

- Learn to know your wife's physical and psychological makeup as an individual woman. What pleases her? What kind of emotional and physical stimulation aids her in being sexually satisfied?

  Caution: What may please your wife on one occasion may not on another. Futhermore, what pleases other women may not necessarily please your wife. Remember, too, that a woman is not as consistent in her response to certain stimuli as men. Don't let this confuse you or threaten you. Accept it as a challenge and learn to know the many moods of your wife and her uniqueness as a woman.

Do I know and understand what my wife is feeling?

This is basic to feminine sexual response. Feelings of resentment, anger, insecurity, fear, etc., are all great inhibitors in causing a woman not to respond sexually.

Listen to your wife's feelings. Encourage her to share how she feels. Accept those feelings. Try not to take personally her negative feelings toward you as a husband. Periodically, these are normal and natural feelings. Though it is sometimes painful, remember that she will love you for accepting her negative feelings and responding with understanding.

How can I be more tender toward my wife?

Mort Katz in his *Marriage Survival Kit*[1] suggests the following to help you develop this quality in your marital relationship:

- Tenderness is asking your wife what she is feeling.
- Tenderness is asking your wife what she means.
- Tenderness is telling your wife that you understand how she feels.
- Tenderness is telling your wife you are glad for her happiness when she is happy.
- Tenderness is telling your wife you are sorry for her pain when she's hurting inside.
- Tenderness is hugging your wife apart from sexual relationships.
- Tenderness is holding your wife gently when she's hurting.
- Tenderness is sharing your happy feelings with your wife.
- Tenderness is tuning into your wife's true feelings.

How can I become more physically attractive to my wife?

It is true that men are far more easily aroused sexually through what they see, but women also find it difficult to be aroused by a physically unattractive husband. The same basic suggestions given to wives also apply to you in making yourself physically more attractive.

- Get rid of excessive weight.
- Bathe regularly.
- Smell good.

And remember: Don't let it threaten you if your wife is not as sexually aroused by your physical manner as you are aroused by her feminine mystique.

WARNING: With the easy accessibility of pornographic movies on video, some Christian couples are utilizing these explicit films as a means of sexual stimulation. This kind of behavior is destructive for several reasons:

- *It is spiritually destructive.*
  Watching men and women engage in fornication, adultery, group sex and homosexual acts (which are the primary activities in pornographic films) is out of the will of God. In essence, this kind of behavior could be the same as if New Testament Christians continued to visit pagan temples to watch temple prostitutes engage in all kinds of sexual behavior with their clients.

- *It is psychologically destructive.*
  Though initially stimulating, pornography very quickly loses its emotional impact. The fact is it takes more and more explicit and varying material to cause the same sexual responses over a period of time. Because of their visual orientation, this is particularly true of men. Over a period of time, this kind of experience can lead to impotence.

- *It is ultimately destructive in a marital relationship.*
  Pornography is particularly threatening to women, especially if she senses her husband is dependent on this kind of stimulation to be fulfilled sexually. This is a direct statement to his wife that she is not, in herself, attractive enough to create sexual desire in her husband.

An Exercise in Developing Sexual Love

As you begin this process as a couple, your greatest challenge is being sensitive in the communication that lies before you. You're venturing into the most vulnerable area of your inner being. Be honest, yet kind and gentle. Remember, too, that if you find you do not measure up in these areas as you thought you would or as you hoped to, it will be a great opportunity for developing both understanding and skill as a sexual partner. Though you may be initially threatened, great dividends can eventually come.

Note: If you reach an impasse in communication, you may need to seek help from an objective third party who is skilled in marital counseling.

Step 1—Instructions for Both Spouses

Complete the following "Evaluation Scale for Wives" and the "Evaluation Scale for Husbands."

Step 1—Scale 1: An Evaluation Scale for Wives

The following statements are designed to help you discover how much you know about your husband's sexual nature and needs and what you are doing to meet those needs. Circle the number that best describes how you view your sexual relationship with your husband.

	Not at all				Very much
1. I understand and accept my husband's sexual nature, such as:					
a. His visual orientation;	1	2	3	4	5
b. His tendency to be easily sexually aroused;	1	2	3	4	5
c. His glandular makeup	1	2	3	4	5
d. The close relationship between his self-image and my attitudes toward his sexual physiology.	1	2	3	4	5
2. I am quite aware of my husband's sexual temptations.	1	2	3	4	5
3. I am understanding and accepting of my husband's sexual temptations.	1	2	3	4	5
4. I make an effort to be available to my husband sexually even when my sexual desires are low.	1	2	3	4	5
5. I give attention to making myself physically attractive to my husband by:					
a. Controlling my weight;	1	2	3	4	5
b. Bathing before lovemaking;	1	2	3	4	5
c. Using cosmetics effectively;	1	2	3	4	5
d. Dressing appropriately for the bedroom.	1	2	3	4	5
6. I try to be a creative lover by:					
a. At times initiating our lovemaking;	1	2	3	4	5

(over)

   b. Introducing variety into sexual
     form;   1 2 3 4 5
   c. Thinking of unique ways to set the
     stage for lovemaking;   1 2 3 4 5
   d. Helping to add variety to the
     place where we make love.   1 2 3 4 5

7. I set a good stage for lovemaking by:
   a. Keeping the bedroom neat and
     attractive;   1 2 3 4 5
   b. Establishing a positive emotional
     environment;   1 2 3 4 5

8. I try to meet my husband's sexual
   needs creatively even when it is
   inconvenient for me because of
   pregnancy, menstrual periods, etc.; 1 2 3 4 5

9. I have learned to say no without
   threatening my husband when I
   desire to postpone any form of lovemaking.   1 2 3 4 5

10. I look for the next natural opportunity
    to make love when I have asked to
    postpone lovemaking.   1 2 3 4 5

11. I know, understand and accept what
    my husband likes and dislikes about
    lovemaking.   1 2 3 4 5

12. I make it easy for my husband to talk
    about our sexual relationship. 1 2 3 4 5

Step 1—Scale 1: An Evaluation Scale for Husbands

The following statements are designed to help you discover how much you know about your wife's sexual nature and needs and what you are doing to meet those needs. Circle the number that best describes how you view your sexual relationship with your wife.

	Not at all				Very much
1. I understand and accept my wife's sexual nature, such as:					
a. What factors cause her to be sexually aroused;	1	2	3	4	5
b. What factors make the total sexual experience desirable for her;	1	2	3	4	5
c. The way her menstrual cycle affects her sexual drives;	1	2	3	4	5
d. Her need to feel she is an adequate sexual partner.	1	2	3	4	5
2. I am aware of how my wife's sexual nature is different from my own.	1	2	3	4	5
3. I understand my wife's feelings in relationship to sexual response.	1	2	3	4	5
4. I make myself available to my wife in a variety of ways other than sex.	1	2	3	4	5
5. I give attention to making myself physically attractive to my wife by:					
a. Controlling my weight;	1	2	3	4	5
b. Bathing before lovemaking;	1	2	3	4	5
c. Using pleasant body lotions effectively;	1	2	3	4	5
d. Careful grooming (close shave, well-manicured nails, etc.)	1	2	3	4	5
6. I try to be a creative lover by:					
a. Giving my wife opportunity at times to initiate lovemaking;	1	2	3	4	5

(over)

    b. Initiating variety into sexual form;   1 2 3 4 5
    c. Thinking of unique ways to set the
       stage for lovemaking;   1 2 3 4 5
    d. Helping to add variety to the
       place where we make love.   1 2 3 4 5

7. I set a good stage for lovemaking by:
    a. Helping my wife with household
       chores, which will make it possi-
       ble for her to be both physically
       and emotionally available for love-
       making;   1 2 3 4 5
    b. Establishing a positive emotional
       environment.   1 2 3 4 5

8. I accept my wife's efforts to satisfy
    me sexually when her participation is
    limited because of pregnancy, men-
    struation, etc.   1 2 3 4 5

9. I accept my wife's feelings without
    reacting negatively when she wishes
    to postpone lovemaking.   1 2 3 4 5

10. I look for opportunities to express
    affection to my wife apart from sexual
    activity.   1 2 3 4 5

11. I make it easy for my wife to talk
    about our sexual relationship.   1 2 3 4 5

12. I understand the nature of my wife's
    sexual temptations and how they dif-
    fer from my own.

Step 2—Instructions for Both Spouses

Now that you have completed the evaluation scales designed for each of you (Scale 1), complete the following comparative scales (Scale 2).

Step 2—Scale 2: An Evaluation Exercise for Wives About Their Husbands

The following exercise is designed for you to communcia-te your perspective on how you feel your husband relates to you sexually.

	Not at all			Very much

1. My husband understands and accepts my sexual nature, such as:
   a. What factors cause me to be sexually aroused; 1 2 3 4 5
   b. What factors make the total sexual experience desirable for me; 1 2 3 4 5
   c. How my menstrual cycles affect my sexual drive; 1 2 3 4 5
   d. My need to feel that I'm adequate as a sexual partner. 1 2 3 4 5
2. My husband knows how to help me respond sexually. 1 2 3 4 5
3. My husband understands my feelings and how they relate to my sexual response. 1 2 3 4 5
4. My husband makes himself available to me in a variety of ways other than sex. 1 2 3 4 5
5. My husband gives attention to making himself physically attractive by:
   a. Controlling his weight; 1 2 3 4 5
   b. Bathing before lovemaking; 1 2 3 4 5
   c. Using pleasant body lotions effectively; 1 2 3 4 5
   d. Careful grooming (close shave, well manicured nails, etc.) 1 2 3 4 5
6. My husband tries to be a creative lover by:

(over)

    a. Giving me opportunity at times to
       initiate lovemaking;   1 2 3 4 5
    b. Initiating variety into sexual form; 1 2 3 4 5
    c. Thinking of unique ways to set the
       stage for lovemaking;   1 2 3 4 5
    d. Helping to add variety to the
       place where we make love.   1 2 3 4 5

 7. My husband sets a good stage for
    lovemaking by:
    a. Helping me with household
       chores that will make it possible
       for me to be both physically and
       emotionally available for lovemak-
       ing;   1 2 3 4 5
    b. Establishing a positive emotional
       environment.   1 2 3 4 5

 8. My husband accepts my efforts to
    satisfy him sexually when my partici-
    pation is limited because of preg-
    nancy, menstruation, etc.   1 2 3 4 5

 9. My husband accepts my feelings
    without reacting negatively when I
    wish to postpone lovemaking.   1 2 3 4 5

10. My husband looks for opportunities
    to express affection to me apart from
    sexual activity.   1 2 3 4 5

11. My husband makes it easy for me to
    talk about our sexual relationship. 1 2 3 4 5

12. My husband understands the nature
    of my sexual temptations and how
    they differ from his.   1 2 3 4 5

Step 2—Scale 2: An Evaluation Exercise for Husbands About Their Wives

The following exercise is designed for you to communicate your perspective on how you feel your wife relates to you sexually.

	Not at all				Very much

1. My wife understands and accepts my sexual nature, such as:
   a. My visual orientation;   1 2 3 4 5
   b. My tendency to be easily sexually aroused;   1 2 3 4 5
   c. My glandular makeup;   1 2 3 4 5
   d. The close relationship between my self-image and her attitudes toward my sexual physiology.   1 2 3 4 5
2. My wife is quite aware of my sexual temptations.   1 2 3 4 5
3. My wife is understanding and accepting of my sexual temptations.   1 2 3 4 5
4. My wife makes an effort to be available to me sexually even when her sexual desires are low.   1 2 3 4 5
5. My wife gives attention to making herself physically attractive to me by:
   a. Controlling her weight;   1 2 3 4 5
   b. Bathing before lovemaking;   1 2 3 4 5
   c. Using cosmetics effectively;   1 2 3 4 5
   d. Dressing appropriately for the bedroom.   1 2 3 4 5
6. My wife tries to be a creative lover by:
   a. At times initiating our lovemaking;   1 2 3 4 5
   b. Introducing variety into sexual form;   1 2 3 4 5
   c. Thinking of unique ways to

(over)

     c. set the stage for lovemaking;   1 2 3 4 5
     d. Helping to add variety to the
        place where we make love.   1 2 3 4 5

7. My wife sets a good stage for lovemaking by:
   a. Keeping the bedroom neat and
     attractive;   1 2 3 4 5
   b. Establishing a positive emotional
     environment.   1 2 3 4 5

8. My wife tries to creatively meet my
   sexual needs even when it is inconvenient for her because of pregnancy, menstrual periods, etc.   1 2 3 4 5

9. My wife has learned to say no without
   threatening me when she desires to
   postpone any form of lovemaking.   1 2 3 4 5

10. My wife looks for the next natural
    opportunity to make love when she
    has asked to postpone lovemaking.   1 2 3 4 5

11. My wife knows, understands and
    accepts what I like and dislike about
    lovemaking.   1 2 3 4 5

12. My wife makes it easy for me to talk
    about our sexual relationship.   1 2 3 4 5

Step 3—Instructions for Both Spouses

Record the scores from Scales 1 and 2 in the appropriate columns on the following forms (Scale 3) entitled "A Wife's Comparative Study" and "A Husband's Comparative Study."

Step 3—Scale 3: A Wife's Comparative Study

This exercise is for you to record your numerical responses to Scale 1 in Step 1 and your husband's numerical responses to Scale 2 in Step 2. Record both sets of numbers in the proper columns.

	Scale 1 Wife's Evaluation of Her Own Behavior	Scale 2 Husband's Evaluation of Wife's Behavior
1. Understanding of husband's sexual nature, such as:		
__ a. His visual orientation;	_____	_____
__ b. His tendency to be easily sexually aroused;	_____	_____
__ c. His glandular makeup;	_____	_____
__ d. The close relationship between his self-image and your attitudes toward his sexual physiology.	_____	_____
__ 2. Awareness of husband's sexual temptations.	_____	_____
__ 3. Understanding and accepting of your husband's temptations.	_____	_____
__ 4. Making an effort to be available to your husband sexually even when your sexual desires are low.	_____	_____

(over)

5. Giving attention to making yourself physically attractive to your husband by:

— a. Controlling your weight; _____ _____

— b. Bathing before lovemaking; _____ _____

— c. Using cosmetics effectively; _____ _____

— d. Dressing appropriately for the bedroom. _____ _____

6. Trying to be a creative lover by:

— a. At times initiating lovemaking; _____ _____

— b. Introducing variety into sexual form; _____ _____

— c. Thinking of unique ways to set the stage for lovemaking; _____ _____

— d. Helping to add variety to the place where you make love. _____ _____

7. Setting a good stage for lovemaking by:

— a. Keeping the bedroom neat and attractive; _____ _____

— b. Establishing a positive emotional environment. _____ _____

— 8. Trying to creatively meet your husband's sexual needs even when it is inconvenient

(continued)

    for you because of
pregnancy, menstrual
periods, etc.   —————   —————

__ 9. Learning to say no
without threatening
your husband when
you desire to postpone
any form of lovemak-
ing.   —————   —————

__10. Looking for the next
natural opportunity to
make love when you
have asked to post-
pone lovemaking.   —————   —————

__11. Knowing, understand-
ing and accepting
what your husband
likes and dislikes
about lovemaking.   —————   —————

__12. Making it easy for your
husband to talk about
your sexual relation-
ship.   —————   —————

Step 3—Scale 3: A Husband's Comparative Study

This exercise is for you to record your numerical responses to Scale 1 in Step 1 and your wife's numerical responses to Scale 2 in Step 2. Record both sets of numbers in the proper columns.

	Scale 1 Husband's Evaluation of His Own Behavior	Scale 2 Wife's Evaluation of Husband's Behavior
1. Understanding of wife's sexual nature, such as:		
__ a. What factors cause her to be sexually aroused;	_____	_____
__ b. What factors make the total sexual experience desirable for her;	_____	_____
__ c. The way her menstrual cycle affects her sexual drives;	_____	_____
__ d. Her need to feel she is an adequate sexual partner.	_____	_____
__ 2. Awareness of how wife's sexual nature is different from your own.	_____	_____
__ 3. Understanding wife's feelings in relationship to sexual response.	_____	_____
__ 4. Making yourself available to your wife in a variety of ways other than sex.	_____	_____

(over)

5. Giving attention to making yourself physically attractive to your wife by:

— a. Controlling your weight; _____ _____

— b. Bathing before lovemaking; _____ _____

— c. Using pleasant body lotions effectively; _____ _____

— d. Careful grooming (close shave, well manicured nails, etc.) _____ _____

6. Trying to be a creative lover by:

— a. Giving your wife opportunity at times to initiate lovemaking; _____ _____

— b. Initiating variety into sexual form; _____ _____

— c. Thinking of unique ways to set the stage for lovemaking; _____ _____

— d. Helping to add variety to the place where you make love. _____ _____

7. Setting a good stage for lovemaking by:

— a. Helping your wife with household chores, which will make it possible for her to be both

(continued)

physically and
emotionally avail-
able for lovemak-
ing;   _____   _____
— 　b　Establishing a posi-
tive emotional envi-
ronment.   _____   _____
— 8. Accepting your wife's
efforts to satisfy you
sexually when her par-
ticipation is limited
because of preg-
nancy, menstruation,
etc.   _____   _____
— 9. Accepting your wife's
feelings without react-
ing negatively when
she wishes to post-
pone lovemaking.   _____   _____
—10. Looking for opportuni-
ties to express affec-
tion to your wife apart
from sexual activity.   _____   _____
—11. Making it easy for your
wife to talk about your
sexual relationship.   _____   _____
—12. Understanding the
nature of your wife's
sexual temptations
and how they differ
from your own.   _____   _____

Step 4—Instructions for Both Spouses

Using the comparative studies you've just completed, isolate areas of agreement and disagreement. Place a plus (+) in the space before each item you agree on. Place a minus (-) in each space where you disagree. *Note:* A one-point variance on a five-point scale is usually significant.

Step 5—Instructions for Both Spouses

Sensitively discuss with each other what your areas of disagreement are and why these areas exist. To help you understand each other better, go back and read the information that corresponds with these areas.

Note: If you cannot work through this process satisfactorily, arriving at a degree of mutual understanding and concern for each other, you will probably benefit greatly from some personal counseling from your pastor or another competent counselor.

Step 6:—Instructions for Both Spouses

On the basis of your observations and discussions together, write out at least five personal goals to enable each of you to be better sexual partners.

Step 6—Personal Goals for Wives

I will become a better sexual partner to my husband by:

1.

2.

3

4

5.

Step 6—Personal Goals for Husbands

I will become a better sexual partner to my wife by:

1.

2.

3

4

5.

Step 7—Instructions for Both Spouses

Conclude this process together by participating in a positive interaction exercise suggested by David and Vera Mace in their excellent book entitled, *How to Have a Happy Marriage.*[2]

Sit facing each other and hold hands. Tell each other some of the things that you really appreciate about each other.

Instead of a back-and-forth dialogue, decide who will go first, then take only one turn each. Look into each other's eyes while you talk and address each other directly by name. Do the exercise in a reflective, unhurried way, with pauses wherever you like. During your turn, think of a number of qualities in your partner and share them slowly one by one, beginning each with "I love you because . . . "; or "I like you when . . . "; "Another thing I especially like about you is . . . "; or similar words that come naturally to you.

Take plenty of time with this exercise, and talk about it afterward—how you felt, how you reacted to what was said to you. Furthermore, once you have gone through this experience, do it again from time to time—not often enough to make it routine, but as something to be reserved for special occasions.

Step 8—Instructions for Both Spouses

As a couple, conclude this study together by using Paul's words to the Philippians as a prayer.

> May we have the same attitude in ourselves which was in Christ Jesus, who, although He existed in the form of God, did not regard equality with God a thing to be grasped, but emptied Himself, taking the form of a bond-servant, and being made in the likeness of men. And being found in appearance as a man, He humbled Himself by becoming obe-

dient to the point of death, even death on a cross.
(Phil. 2:5-8 paraphrase)

Just a Beginning

Though we've reached the end of this study, it is really just a beginning. Growing in a marriage relationship must be continuous and ongoing. In fact, it would be well for you to actually start over again and work through all the projects once more. You'll discover that your life together can deepen indefinitely.

Better yet, share the process with someone else. As a couple, start a marriage enrichment class for other couples. This will give you an opportunity to go through the projects once again and to share your insights with the group you're leading.

May your growth as a couple be continually blessed and nurtured by His love and guidance.

Notes
1. Adapted from Mort Katz, *Marriage Survival Kit* (New York: Farnsworth Publishing Company, Inc., 1974), p. 61. Used by permission.
2. David and Vera Mace, *How to Have a Happy Marriage* (Nashville: Abingdon Press, 1977), p. 126. Used by permission.

THE BIBLICAL RENEWAL SERIES
by
Gene A. Getz

ONE ANOTHER SERIES

Building Up One Another
Encouraging One Another
Loving One Another
Praying for One Another
Serving One Another

THE MEASURE OF SERIES

Measure of a . . .
  Church
  Family
  Man
  Woman

PERSONALITY SERIES

When You're Confused and Uncertain (Abraham)
When You Feel Rejected (Joseph)
When Your Goals Seem Out of Reach (Nehemiah)
When the Job Seems Too Big (Joshua)
When You Feel Like a Failure (David)
When the Pressure's On (Elijah)
When You Feel You Haven't Got It (Moses)

BIBLE BOOK SERIES

Pressing on When You'd Rather Turn Back
(Philippians)
Saying No When You'd Rather Say Yes
(Titus)
Believing God When You Are Tempted to Doubt
(James 1)
Doing Your Part When You'd Rather Let God Do It All
(James 2-5)
Looking Up When You Feel Down
(Ephesians 1-3)
Living for Others When You'd Rather Live for Yourself
(Ephesians 4-6)
Standing Firm When You'd Rather Retreat
(1 Thessalonians)

Partners for Life: Making a Marriage That Lasts